Praise for *How to Think Philosophically*

Professor Hall's work is not just an introduction or guide to philosophy as an academic discipline, but an excellent guide to how to live philosophically. Bringing in ancient Greek philosophy (particularly Plato) and Buddhist philosophy (sticking close to the Buddha himself) also provides a multicultural richness not generally found in such a concise introductory text. Highly recommended for students but really for anyone interested in some of the ways that philosophy can help us live intellectually richer, morally better, and generally more fulfilling lives.

—Eric Bain-Selbo, dean of the College of Humanities and Social Sciences, Southeast Missouri State University, and author of *The End(s) of Religion: A History of How the Study of Religion Makes Religion Irrelevant*

Writing in the tradition of Pierre Hadot but with a voice and perspective honed by decades of undergraduate teaching, W. David Hall makes a compelling case for the value of philosophy as a fundamentally human endeavor whose goal is to avoid self-deception and attune one's life to reality. Hall writes in an engaging prose style that provides lucid summaries of major philosophical schools and figures without ever getting bogged down or losing track of his larger theme: that the human capacity for self-delusion makes philosophy necessary. The result is a clearly structured volume that packs a wealth of content and insight into a concise frame. It will be a helpful and timely guide to living and thinking philosophically for anyone who wonders how to live a good and meaningful life—especially in a cultural moment when the ability to distinguish truth from falsehood is severely strained.

—Maria Antonaccio, professor of religious ethics, Bucknell University, and author of *A Philosophy to Live By: Engaging Iris Murdoch*

How

to

Think

Philosophically

How

to

Think

Philosophically

W. David Hall

FORTRESS PRESS
MINNEAPOLIS

29 28 27 26 25 24   1 2 3 4 5 6 7 8 9

Library of Congress Control Number: 2024005757 (print)

Cover design: Angela Griner
Cover image: photograph provided by the author

Print ISBN: 978-1-5064-8988-9
eBook ISBN: 978-1-5064-8989-6

For Lori

Contents

Introduction: Being Philosophical
and Thinking Philosophically   1

Part 1: Being Philosophical

1. Philosophy as a Way of Living   11

2. Asking the Right Questions: The Form
   of the Philosophical Life   21

3. Seeing Things as They Are: The Goal
   of the Philosophical Life   35

4. Attuning to the Way Things Are: The End
   of the Philosophical Life   51

Part 2: Thinking Philosophically

5. Being, Teaching, Thinking   77

6. Epistemology: What Is Knowledge?
   How Do We Know? How Much Can We Know?   89

7. Metaphysics: What Is There? Why Is It There?
   How Does It Work?   115

8. Ethics: Good and Bad, Right and Wrong,
   Moral and Immoral   137

CONTENTS

Conclusion: Thinking Philosophically
and Being Philosophical   169

Bibliography   173

Index   179

Introduction

Being Philosophical and Thinking Philosophically

There is no doubt about it, humans are odd cats. On the one hand, we are driven to ask questions about reality; we wonder about the nature of the world around us, about the meaning of our own lives, and how we should live. We have been blessed (or cursed) with a cognitive apparatus that can push that questioning very far, indeed. So far as we have evidence, we are the only beings in the universe who are capable of asking questions about that universe and our place in it. Our closest animal ancestors, the great apes, organize their lives around complex social relationships, like we do; some species of Cetaceans—whales and dolphins—develop complex ways of communicating within and across species, like we do; Corvids—crows and jays—can use tools to manipulate their environments for their advantage, like we can. But, as far as we can tell, no other being on earth seems driven, let alone able, to raise questions about the fundamental nature of reality. As likely as the existence of other intelligent civilizations in the universe may be, we have not encountered them yet, so we seem alone with our drive and our ability to question. These urges and capabilities make philosophy possible.

On the other hand, humans have a remarkable capacity to deceive themselves about the nature of reality. We often fall back on "common sense," that deposit of conventional wisdom that everybody knows, "without question," to be true. And, while common sense is not always wrong, many have suggested that an uncritical acceptance of conventional wisdom often leads to creative cul-de-sacs, intellectual blind spots, and destructive habits. Often, reliance on unquestioned truths leads us to imagine reality as we would like it to be rather than see it as it is; our actions reflect the determination to make the universe conform to our desires—almost always a losing proposition—rather than the determination to conform our desires and our actions to the ineluctable realities of the way things are. Philosophers have always argued that this uniquely human tendency to deceive ourselves about the nature of things makes philosophy necessary.

What, then, is philosophy? I assume, given the fact that you are perusing the introduction of a book titled *How to Think Philosophically*, that you, my reader, have at least a passing interest in this question. Those who know Greek, the language most commonly associated with the emergence of philosophy in the Western world, will recognize that "philosophy" (*philosophia*) means "love of wisdom." What constitutes wisdom is a matter of dispute among those engaged in the philosophical endeavor (and we will have opportunity to address a number of competing visions of wisdom), but, speaking quite literally, a philosopher is a lover of wisdom, one who takes wisdom as her guide and aims to make wisdom the foundation of her life. Perhaps the better definition for a philosopher is a "seeker of wisdom," given that, for the majority of those who take up this endeavor, the goal of a life of wisdom is continually sought and only partially achieved. Wisdom is elusive and easily misplaced among the cares that confront us in daily life.

The perpetualness of the search and the incompleteness of attainment mark the distinction between the *philosopher* who loves or seeks the life of wisdom and the *sage* who lives it. The philosopher commits herself to the possibly endless search for genuine wisdom and the improbable hope of becoming a true sage. (Socrates, the figure most closely associated with the emergence of Western philosophy, to the end of his life claimed to know nothing, a claim we will interrogate later.) As such, the philosopher cuts a strange figure in the world. Pierre Hadot, a historian of philosophy, explains:

> Now we have a better understanding of the *atopia*, the strangeness of the philosopher in the human world. One does not know how to classify him, for he is neither a sage nor a man like other men. He knows that the normal, natural state of men should be wisdom, for wisdom is nothing more than the vision of things as they are, the vision of the cosmos as it is in the light of reason, and wisdom is also nothing more than the mode of being and living that should correspond to this vision. But the philosopher also knows that this wisdom is an ideal state, almost inaccessible.[1]

The philosopher is *atopos*, out-of-place, neither common (caught up in the ordinary worries of ordinary people) nor extraordinary (achieving the status of sagely existence), hopelessly uncommon.

Anybody who has taken a philosophy class or read a philosophy book will recognize the general weirdness that philosophers truck in. If we look at philosophy as a discipline represented in the curriculum of most colleges and universities, one wonders what possible relevance it could have to the aim of living a successful life. Philosophy is terribly impractical, preoccupied with strange questions and abstract realities, composed of opaque concepts and esoteric languages; heaven forbid that anybody should choose philosophy as a college major. When students step into my introductory philosophy classes, they rarely have any idea what philosophy is about, but they typically are well-versed in the opinion that philosophy is irrelevant, impractical, abstract, esoteric, etc. And, to be honest, philosophy, as it is presented as a discipline in the college and university curriculum, looks pretty strange and impractical. At the institution where I teach, the philosophy curriculum is split into subgenres: history of philosophy, metaphysics and epistemology, and value theory. So, our students know that they are going to be taking courses dealing with some mostly dead, mostly white, mostly guys (though the

3

primarily European-male philosophical cast is happily changing); or they will be taking courses dealing with metaphysics and epistemology (whatever these are); or they will be taking courses about how to be a good person (which most think they already know). The truth is that philosophers are not always the best advocates for what they do.

Some of the problem is the tendency to think of philosophy as a particular kind of academic discipline, that is, as a particular set of questions approached from a particular set of methodologies using a particular professional language. Certainly, philosophy involves a peculiar way of engaging reality, a distinct method of thinking and questioning, but this methodological aspect is secondary to the more existential aspect of *being philosophical*. While philosophers in ancient Greece organized themselves into various schools of thought, those philosophy "schools" were not organized around a set of well-defined disciplines—like academic departments: art history, biology, economics, etc.—but usually focused on the teachings of a founding figure. Those founding figures became famous and attracted students because they offered a compelling account of wisdom, that is, a reasoned account of the nature of reality that, if adopted, became not just an understanding of the universe, but entailed, as well, a way of living. Thus, at its origins, philosophy was not so much *a discipline* in our sense of the term—a particular method or set of methods for exploring particular aspects of the world—as *discipline*, in a more robust sense; philosophy started off as the advocation of a way of living that involved spiritual and intellectual exercises which, if mastered, promised to create a certain kind of personality, a way of life, a way of being in the world. To put it succinctly, *being philosophical is a manner of inhabiting the world in an intentional way, such that one asks questions and seeks to understand the way things are, in order to attune one's life to reality.* If we accept this as a basic definition of what it means to live philosophically, then we are all philosophers on some level, whether we realize it or not, whether we like it or not. We all want to understand how to live meaningful lives, the ultimate end of philosophy.

If there is anything that makes self-identified philosophers unique, it is that they make the task of living a meaningful life their primary focus, and part of this focus usually entails convincing others to be a bit more reflective about the task of living. Generally speaking, philosophers do not want to make only their own lives better, they want to make others' lives better, too. It is a matter of making others more intentional in their living. Corresponding to this basic way of being philosophical, then, is a distinct way of *thinking philosophically*. This peculiar way of thinking and speaking is typically what people associate with philosophy. I will argue that *thinking* philosophically is secondary to, and derived from, the more basic existential orientation of *being* philosophical. Philosophers often speak of the importance of thinking systematically or analytically. What this means, broadly understood, is that one ought to be methodical in one's thinking; thinking philosophically is a process of critical engagement with problems. We need to address the characteristics of this process of critical engagement.

First and foremost, philosophers are skeptics. Recall that one of the arguments for the necessity of philosophy is the uniquely human tendency for self-deception, and one of the principal causes of self-deception is the uncritical willingness to accept conventional accounts of the nature of things. In this sense, philosophers are skeptical on principle; they ask questions that nobody else would think to ask about things that everyone assumes to be settled and understood. If the goal is to understand reality for what it is and to avoid the deception of seeing things as we would like them to be, then nothing is out of the question.

Second, philosophers aim to be rational in their engagements and their conclusions. It is important to define rationality capaciously. This broad notion of rationality entails that we ought to have reasons for holding our beliefs about reality, reasons that we could articulate and would be willing to defend when called to account. And, perhaps most importantly, we ought to be willing to reformulate our beliefs if there seem to be good reasons to do so. One problem with conventional wisdom is that it is often accepted without thought, and without any intellectual defense. Worst of all, the defenders of common sense are rarely willing to change their views when there seem to be good reasons to do so. (Defenders of convention are the frequent targets of philosophical criticism.)

Finally, philosophers place great weight on being logical. Here again, logic is defined broadly. There is a formal study of logic, and this study is important training in thinking generally, but I intend logical thinking in a wider sense than this. Logic is the methodical aspect of philosophical thinking. We will have opportunity to address this aspect of thinking *philosophically*—that is, skeptically, rationally, and logically—later.

This book is structured around the two poles of *being philosophical* and *thinking philosophically*. Part 1 deals with the existential question of what it means to live a philosophical life. Chapter 1 lays out what this philosophical existence entails. In thinking about philosophy as a way of life, I suggest that that form of life is anchored by two kinds of cognitive endeavor, or two intellectual virtues: (1) becoming aware of how much you do not know, or "learning to be dumb in the right way," and (2) being curious about things others might not notice, or "wondering." These two intellectual orientations fuel the philosophical life; learning to be dumb about things leads one to wonder about a great many things, even things that are supposedly commonplace. And, being curious leads to asking questions in hopes of seeing things as they are so that one can organize one's life correctly.

Chapter 2 focuses on figuring out how to ask the right questions with the goal of becoming aware of how much one does not know. Humans tend to think they know more than they do, and much of this tendency is due to the fact that they accept and defend inherited answers to questions. The first step in being philosophical is to raise questions about those inherited answers to test whether they really stand up to scrutiny. This practice tends to make philosophers unpopular because they question the validity of much of what others hold to be unquestionable. Being philosophical is first and foremost the endeavor not to take anything for granted.

The tendency not to take things for granted and to ask questions about what seems to be unquestionable makes the philosophical life a curious one. In one sense, philosophers look curious (read peculiar and perhaps dangerous) because they ask questions that make others uncomfortable. In another sense, however, philosophers are just curious; they wonder about things that others do not. This notion is the meaning behind Socrates's dictum that philosophy "begins in wonder." The goal of philosophy is to see things the way they are rather than the way we would like them to be, and this requires wondering about how things *really* are. This quest to understand reality is the focus of chapter 3.

An aspect of the philosophical life that has been frequently forgotten is that the goal of philosophy is not just to learn how to ask the right questions in order to see things for the way they are. The ultimate end is to learn how to live in consonance with the way things are, the focus of chapter 4. There are many examples of this endeavor in the history of philosophy. Stoic philosophers, for instance, argued that the universe is guided by an overarching logic, the *logos*; the goal of philosophy is to come to an understanding of the *logos* so as to learn to live in conformity with it. I will conclude that any systematic philosophical engagement with reality has (or ought to have) this ultimate end of learning how to live well.

Part 2 of the volume shifts gears and takes up the kind of thinking and questioning that corresponds to this way of living. The second part of the book addresses these issues by comparing two philosophical approaches with very different cultural backgrounds and histories: Platonism and Buddhism. Chapter 5 draws the connection between being philosophical and thinking philosophically. It lays out the principal subdivisions in the study of philosophy: epistemology—the science of knowledge; metaphysics—accounts of the ultimate nature of reality; and ethics—how to live well. It also lays out the trajectory of the rest of the volume: a conversation between Platonism and Buddhism. The former is one of the major positions in the history of philosophy, and the latter, often thought of as a religion, is a perspective that is philosophical to its core.

Chapter 6 addresses philosophical accounts of knowledge: episte-mology. The subfield of epistemology aims to give some account of what knowledge is, how we come to know, and the degree to which we can know. The chapter lays out the fundamental aims of episte-mology, and these aims will be fleshed out by comparing the Socratic method and its relation to Platonism with the Buddhist understand-ings of experience and meditation as modes of understanding.

Chapter 7 addresses philosophical accounts of the nature of real-ity: metaphysics. The goal of metaphysics is to chart the distinction between the way things appear and the way things are. Every branch of metaphysics recognizes that there is a relation between the way things appear and the way they really are; in some cases, the differ-ence between the two is distant, in others it is quite close. The chap-ter fleshes out the importance of metaphysics by comparing Plato's theory of Forms with the Buddhist distinction between conventional reality and ultimate reality.

Chapter 8 addresses philosophical accounts of the good life: ethics. Ethics addresses the question of how we ought to live. Ethics is where "the rubber meets the road" in philosophy. Staying with the ultimate trajectory of the volume, the goal of philosophy is to learn how to live. After addressing several of the dominant ethical theories in the history of philosophy—virtue, consequentialism, rule-based, or deontological ethics—the chapter focuses on Plato's understanding of the Form of the Good in comparison with the Buddhist doctrine of the eightfold path. In the conclusion of the volume we will return to the relationship between being and thinking.

NOTE

1 Pierre Hadot, *Philosophy as a Way of Life*, trans. Michael Chase, ed. Arnold I. Davidson (Malden, MA: Blackwell, 1995), 58.

PART ONE

Being Philosophical

CHAPTER ONE

Philosophy as a Way of Living

Those who have been branded with the epithet "philosopher," or who have been foolhardy enough to self-identify as such, approach things in a weird way. They tend to question things that are usually taken for granted, and they often seem to take glee in making others feel uncomfortable in doing so. While there may be some native proclivity among philosophers to deal with things this way, make no mistake, being philosophical is a choice, a decision to live in this peculiar way. Speaking of the ancient and Hellenistic philosophers of Greece and Rome (roughly the period from the fourth century BCE through the fourth century CE), Pierre Hadot claims that philosophy "was a way of life, both in its exercise and effort to achieve wisdom, and in its goal, wisdom itself. For real wisdom does not merely cause us to know: it makes us 'be' in a different way."[1] Thus, to commit oneself to the "love of wisdom" meant not only to take up a particular course of study, but to commit oneself to a way of living, a way of being in the world and in oneself.

From the outside, this attachment of philosophy to life is counterintuitive. Philosophy as it has come to be done and taught is, primarily, a professional practice that takes place between professional philosophers and is perpetrated on students in philosophy classrooms. Its primary domain is the ivory towers of the academy. There are reasons for this contemporary separation of philosophy from the everyday, a set of historical circumstances that led to what could be called the professionalization of philosophy. Hadot argues that the split transpired in the Middle Ages as philosophy became the "handmaid" to Christian theology. The Medieval period (roughly from the fifth through the fourteenth century CE) marked the emergence of the institution of the European university and a new guild of scholars, the "Scholastics," engaged in Christian theological speculation. In this period, philosophy became a specialized discourse marshalled in the service of thinking through and articulating Christian concepts and dogmas. Even as philosophy escaped the yoke of theology in the Enlightenment (seventeenth and eighteenth centuries), with rare exceptions, its primary home remained in the university, and its primary mode remained the specialized language developed during the Medieval period.[2] (Other, non-Western, philosophical traditions take their own, different path, a topic we will address in the second part of the book.)

As I suggested in my introduction, however, we are all philosophers at some level. If we focus on the notion that philosophy is the quest for wisdom that commits one to a particular way of life, then philosophy is not a profession or a system of thinking; it is a way of being. It is important to ground *thinking* philosophically in the way of *being* philosophical. The first part of this book attempts to lay out what it means to *be philosophical*.

We can structure this explanation around the ideas of *form, goal*, and *end*. Let's call the form of the philosophical life "learning how to ask the right questions." I tell my students that philosophers ask a lot of questions. Whether those questions have answers is up for grabs, but being philosophical finally means learning to ask the right kinds of questions. And, learning to ask the right kinds of questions involves cultivating what we might call a set of intellectual virtues. I'll call these intellectual virtues (1) learning to be dumb in the right way and (2) wondering about things.

Surely, learning to be dumb is a strange intellectual virtue; if philosophy is the seeking of wisdom, then being dumb seems contrary to the task. The philosopher, however, does not seek to be dumb in just any old way; he wants to become dumb *in the right way*. Indeed, he tends to think, perhaps conceitedly, that most people are dumb in the *wrong* way, and his cultivation of stupidity is of a different sort. The problem philosophers encounter is that humans tend to think they know more than they really do, and a primary source of this delusion is a reliance on conventional wisdom. We are all born into a particular cultural context, and we are brought up in and shaped by our culture's conventional ways of understanding and organizing reality. While these conventions may be fine, in and of themselves, and indeed necessary for negotiating our interactions with others who share that culture, they typically go unquestioned. The unquestioned reliance on conventional wisdom, coupled with the widespread human vanity of wishing to be thought wise, makes people just plain dumb, or so the philosopher argues. He wants to replace this run-of-the-mill stupidity with a more refined form. Call it *the cultivation of a sense of ignorance*: the willingness to place in question what one has been told, to consider whether one knows what he thinks he knows, indeed, to consider the possibility that he knows nothing at all.

This cultivation of ignorance leads to a second intellectual virtue, *wondering about things*. Socrates, is quoted as saying that all philosophizing starts with wonder.[3] We get a sense of this virtue of wondering if we compare it to the conventional wisdom I discussed above. If we trace the origins of conventional ways of thinking about things, they tend to be grounded in the ideas of those, frequently in the past, who thought themselves wise (and perhaps were thought wise by others). Over the course of time, those ideas become detached to some degree from their progenitors to form time-honored traditions that ground our views of the world and our social interactions. Once an idea becomes part of tradition, opinions tend to ossify around it, and it becomes an unquestioned truth. The wondering philosopher tries to trace conventions back to their originating authorities and to question whether those authorities were as wise as they (and perhaps others) thought. She tests the time-honored traditions looking for holes and blind spots. She aims to form her own opinions about the realities that go unquestioned in conventional wisdom. Of course, questions often raise more questions, and if she is truly committed to a life of wisdom-seeking, she is committed to placing in question her own opinions. These facts turn the philosophical life into a kind of perpetual motion machine, a self-perpetuating, never-ending process. However, the philosopher places bets that learning to ask the right questions will pay off in the end with a better understanding of the way things are—the goal of being philosophical—and better prospects for a worthwhile life—the end of the philosophical way of life.

Characterizing the goal of being philosophical as "gaining a better understanding of the way things are" points to the general tendency of philosophers to assume that there is more than meets the eye when it comes to the nature of reality. We have all been in situations where we have experienced a disconnect between appearance and reality, where a deep intuition dawned that there is something going on beneath the surface of things that needs to be explored. If we call the general human tendency to rely unquestioningly on things as they appear "common sense," the philosopher's task to learn to ask the right kinds of questions involves interrogating common sense, along with the conventional wisdom it is typically based on, to dig beneath appearances to get at a more fundamental level of reality behind those appearances, to see things as they *really are.*

Philosophers certainly are not the only odd fellows to question the distinction between appearance and reality. Scientists do this all the time, as do artists and poets in their own way. (Incidentally, science, understood as a form of methodological inquiry distinct from philosophy is a relatively recent development in Western intellectual history. Prior to the seventeenth century or so, the field of disciplines we recognize as the natural sciences would have been thought of as a branch of philosophy.) My conversations with my chemist friends have revealed to me that the desk I sit at as I work on this manuscript, which appears as a solid object, is really mostly empty space. This thing I rest my arms on while I type ideas into my computer is really composed of tiny bits of matter called molecules, that are composed of even smaller bits of matter called atoms. These molecules and atoms are bound together by electrochemical bonds, and the resistance this compound object—called a desk—puts up against my arms, that makes it *feel* like a solid object, is really the electrochemical interactions happening between the atoms and molecules that compose my desk and the atoms and molecules that compose my arms. After all, the solid-appearing object that is me is a product of the same chemical laws as the desk, as is the computer I type into, as is the dogwood tree I can see outside the window, as is the window itself, and so on. My conversations with my physicist friends further complicate things: the atoms that compose the molecules that compose my desk, are composed of even smaller subatomic bits of matter, and some physicists even question whether our understanding of matter is itself just an appearance. (At this point, I have to give a shout-out to my high school chemistry teacher, Mr. Schiermeyer, affectionately known as "Schiermie," for sending me off on this bizarre journey to live a philosophical life. Beside teaching about "mole islands" and the explosive qualities of sodium metal, he convinced me to read Hermann Hesse's novel, *Siddhartha*.)

No doubt, digging beneath the surface of appearances is bewildering, indeed scary. The seventeenth-century philosopher and scientist Blaise Pascal characterized the human condition as being suspended between two abysses, the infinitely large expanse of the universe and the infinitely small reality of the microscopic. Pascal pictured the human as a "thinking reed," a being existing at the crux of an unfathomable expanse that threatens to crush it and an unimaginable microscopic world that, equally, threatens its undoing.[4] (Pascal lived at a time when microbiology was just developing, when our understanding of diseases caused by microorganisms was just forming.) This realization drove him to the precipice of despair, yet Pascal found in this condition an unimpeachable nobility: though the human being is a bending reed, at the mercy of a universe that threatens to blot it out, that universe knows nothing of this situation. The human being is a *thinking* reed, a being that *knows* both itself and the universe, and this ability to know delineates the grandeur of the human in the midst of an unknowing universe.

So, striving to see things as they really are may not be for the weak of stomach. There is a further philosophical claim, however: the ability to situate ourselves better in reality will cash out in finding better ways to live. The end of the philosophical life is not just to gain a better understanding of the way things are, but to *learn how to live a worthwhile life* given the way things are. In some ways, this is just unquestionable (or at least should be), since understanding the way things really are contributes not just to living a *worthwhile* life but maintaining *any life at all*. For instance, if I operate out of a world-view that has, as part of it, the unquestioned belief that all elephants are friendly beasts that like to be hand-fed peanuts, like the ones I encountered at the circus when I was a child, I might be inclined to approach any elephants I encounter and offer them peanuts. It was made manifest to me during a trip to a game preserve in South Africa that not all elephants like to be approached, however. (Fortunately, I had already amended my beliefs about elephants; I watch a lot of nature programs because I am nerdy that way. I have also amended my beliefs about circuses being happy, enchanting places to take your kids, and I am pleased that they are going out of fashion.) I did not wait around to see if all elephants like peanuts. Lessons learned from Pascal: in the face of a charging elephant, I am a bending reed, and it is good to be reminded of this from time to time.

However, the philosopher's claim that understanding the way things are will lead us to a better way of living runs deeper than merely understanding how to preserve our lives in face of charging elephants. Ultimately at stake is how to live a *good* life. The Greek philosopher, Aristotle (384–322 BCE), indicated that, when asked about the nature of the good life, everybody agrees that a good life is a happy life. However, this is where agreement ends, he argued, because disputes over the nature of happiness are many: some say that wealth secures happiness, others that health is the ground of happiness, others argue for good reputation, and so on. Aristotle argued that anything that would constitute happiness must be *final*—the object of happiness must be sought for itself and not for anything else— and *self-sufficient*—possession of the thing must secure happiness, in and of itself, independently of anything else. These requirements disqualify most things that are conventionally taken to secure happiness: wealth is not sought for itself, but to secure other things we want; health and reputation are not self-sufficient as there are many examples of healthy individuals who enjoy the good opinion of others but who are not happy. Aristotle concluded that the only thing that secures a final and self-sufficient happiness is virtue. That is to say, *the happy life is the virtuous life*, the maximal perfection of the catalog of virtues he outlined in the *Nicomachian Ethics*. Only virtue, Aristotle asserted, is sought for itself and secures happiness independent of one's situation.[5]

Virtues, Aristotle argued, come in two types: moral and intellectual. Moral virtues are dispositions or character traits like honesty, courage, and generosity; achieving a morally virtuous life means developing not just one, but all the virtues to the best of one's ability. More important in securing ultimate happiness, however, are the intellectual virtues, those traits that lead to true wisdom. Thus, unsurprisingly, Aristotle characterizes the philosophical life as the truly happy life.[6] So, we circle back to the philosopher's claim that the philosophical life is the best one. There is perhaps some question-begging here, but this is the philosopher's bet, that learning to ask the right kinds of questions leads to a better understanding of the way things are and better prospects for a worthwhile life.

One final insight Aristotle gives us regarding happiness: genuine happiness rests not in one or a few moments, but in the greater balance of happiness to unhappiness over the course of a life, for "just as one swallow does not make a summer, nor does one day; and so too one day, or a short time, does not make a man blessed and happy."[7] There are really two insights encapsulated here. First, life is hard; human existence is full of misfortunes that threaten our happiness. One aim of the philosophical life is to learn how to deal with misfortune, to preserve happiness in the face of perceived evils. No other philosophical school took this aim of learning to deal with misfortune more seriously than the Stoics. The Stoic philosopher, Epictetus (ca. 50–135 CE), claimed that no event is evil, in and of itself; rather our judgments about, and reactions to, the event give it the cast of evil. Most misfortune is beyond our control. The best we can do is live in such a way that we do not bring misfortune upon ourselves—to cultivate virtue—and develop an attitude of indifference toward the bad things that just happen—to recognize them as part of the way things are. In Epictetus's words, when misfortune arises, "examine it by the rules which you possess, and by this first and chiefly, whether it relates to things which are in our power or to things which are not in our power: and if it relates to anything which is not in our power, be ready to say, that it does not concern you."[8] In other words, living well is a matter of distinguishing between the things you can do something about and the things you cannot.

A second, perhaps unsettling, insight we get from Aristotle's statement about the happy life is that we cannot make any final judgments about it while it is in motion. It is impossible to determine whether somebody has lived a happy life until it is over. In some ways this is a truism: a life stream branches into many tributaries, and some of those branches may be catastrophic. Indeed, unless you are born under a lucky star, you will encounter obstacles and your life will take turns that seem to undo the hard work of piecing together a meaningful life. And, one irrevocable destiny awaits us all, the conclusion of that hard work of piecing together, the great unknown, death. There are many philosophical visions of what awaits us on the other side of death, but these are, at best, speculations. One thing that philosophers offer, however, is not just the possibility of a worthwhile life, but also a way not to fear death. After his trial and death sentence, Socrates is reported to have said, "a man who has really devoted his life to philosophy should be cheerful in the face of death, and confident of finding the greatest blessing in the next world when his life is finished"; in short, philosophy is preparation for "dying and death."[9] Epicurus (341–270 BCE), the namesake of the philosophical school famous for grounding the happy life in seeking pleasure and avoiding pain, famously declared that death is "nothing to us . . . . so long as we are existent death is not present and whenever it is present we are nonexistent."[10] Unlike Socrates, Epicurus did not believe there was any life other than this one; death is just the dissolution of life. So, we ought to devote ourselves to enjoying the time we have and not fret over our ultimate demise. Death, for him, literally is nothing. It is the end of being and, thus, release from the whims of fortune and misfortune. However this or that philosopher defines it, living well gives some security that we can die happy, another sense in which living well is the *end* of the philosophical way of life.

In sum, the philosophical way of life is *learning how to ask the right kinds of questions, in order to understand the way things are, so as to attune one's life to the way things are.* The following three chapters will put flesh on the skeleton I have described here. Chapter 2 focuses on the task of learning how to ask the right kinds of questions. Chapter 3 catalogues some of the philosophical answers that have been offered for the way things really are. Chapter 4 addresses some philosophical proposals for how we ought to live.

NOTES

1 Pierre Hadot, *Philosophy as a Way of Life*, trans. Michael Chase, ed. Arnold I. Davidson (Malden, MA: Blackwell Publishing, 1995), 265.

2 Hadot, *Philosophy as a Way of Life*, 269–271.

3 Plato, "Theatetus," 155.d, in *Plato: Collected Dialogues*, trans. Benjamin Jowett, ed. Edith Hamilton and Huntington Cairns (Princeton, NJ: Princeton University Press, 1961), 860.

4 Blaise Pascal, *Pensées*, trans. A. J. Krailsheimer (New York: Penguin Books, 1995), 95.

5 Aristotle, "Nicomachean Ethics," bk. I, ch. 7–8, in *The Basic Works of Aristotle*, ed. Richard McKeon, trans. W. D. Ross (New York: Random House, 1941), 941–945.

6 Aristotle, "Nicomachean Ethics," bk. X, ch. 7, 1104–1105.

7 Aristotle, "Nicomachean Ethics," bk. I, ch. 7, 1098^a: 18–19, 943.

8 Epictetus, *Enchiridion*, trans. George Long (Buffalo: Prometheus Books, 1991), 12.

9 Plato, "Phaedo," 64.a, in *Plato: Collected Dialogues*, trans. Hugh Tredennick, ed. Elizabeth Hamilton and Huntington Cairns (Princeton University Press, 1961), 46.

10 Epicurus, "Letter to Menoeceus," in *The Philosophy of Epicurus*, trans. and ed. George K. Strodach (Evanston, IL: Northwestern University Press, 1963), 180.

CHAPTER TWO

Asking the Right Questions

The Form of the Philosophical Life

STRANGE VIRTUES

The philosophical form of life is peculiar. Recall that Pierre Hadot characterized the philosopher as *atopos*, out of place, uncommon. Philosophers cultivate a peculiar kind of life characterized by constantly questioning common sense and, often, casting off social conventions. In some cases, this peculiarity is quite pronounced. The Cynic philosophers of ancient Greece, for instance, chose a life that made them social outcasts; they became so unconventional that they were not fit for polite company. Hadot explains,

> The Cynic way of life was spectacularly opposed not only to the life of nonphilosophers but even to the lives of other philosophers. . . . They rejected what most people considered the elementary rules and conditions of life in society: cleanliness, pleasant appearance, and courtesy. They practiced deliberate shamelessness—masturbating in public, like Diogenes, or making love in public, like Crates and Hipparchia. The Cynics were absolutely unconcerned with social proprieties and opinions; they despised money, did not hesitate to beg,

and avoided seeking stable positions within the city. They were 'without a city, without a home, without a country, miserable, wandering, living from day to day.' Their bags contained only what was strictly necessary for survival.[1]

Unlike many other philosophers, Cynics did not engage in philosophical argumentation. While they had a minimal set of philosophical doctrines and ideals—self-discipline, independence, adaption to circumstances, simplicity, and, perhaps above all, *parrhesia*, or frank and provocative speech—and developed master–pupil relationships to inculcate their ideals, these doctrines and ideals were not espoused discursively so much as lived out in practice. The Cynics were the lunatic fringe of the ancient philosophical world—kind of like the hardcore hippies (minus the drugs) of the 1960s or the hardcore survivalists (minus the guns) of the twenty-first century; if we put philosophical peculiarity on a continuum that runs from conventionality to "just plain weird," they are on the far end of the weirdness side of the spectrum. However, though the Cynics represent the extreme version of philosophical oddness, most philosophers generally stuck out like sore thumbs in the ancient world. It might be argued that contemporary philosophers retain a bit of this strangeness.

One of the things that makes philosophers peculiar is that they cultivate a strange set of interlocking intellectual virtues. I characterized those virtues as learning to be dumb in the right way and wondering about things others typically do not. Perhaps, a less jarring way to put the first of these virtues is *the cultivation of a sense of ignorance*. The philosopher lives constantly questioning whether she knows what she thinks she knows and, at bottom, whether she knows anything at all. The ability to cultivate this sense of ignorance moves the philosopher to question commonsensical notions and to wonder if they are so commonsensical after all. In this chapter, I hope to flesh out what these intellectual attitudes look like in practice.

CULTIVATING A SENSE OF IGNORANCE

In his defense against charges of impiety and corruption of youth before the court of Athens, Socrates presents the following argument:

> I have gained this reputation, gentlemen, from nothing more or less than a kind of wisdom. What kind of wisdom do I mean? Human wisdom, I suppose. It seems that I really am wise in this limited sense. Presumably the geniuses I mentioned just now are wise in a wisdom that is more than human. I do not know how else to account for it. I certainly have no knowledge of such wisdom, and anyone who says that I have is a liar and willful slanderer.[2]

Socrates claims that the charges of denying the existence of the gods and corrupting the youth of Athens are trumped-up. He is incapable of such actions because he lacks any genuine wisdom. While he may be thought wise in human terms, Socrates places little value on a merely human wisdom. In short, Socrates knows nothing about the gods except what he is told about them, and he lacks any insight that could have a corrupting influence.

Socrates (c. 470–399 BCE) is an interesting character who has entered our discussion at several points already, so it is worthwhile to spend some time explaining who he was. Though he was a notorious figure in ancient Athens, though the ideas ascribed to him are critical in the formation of Western philosophy, Socrates wrote nothing; indeed, by all accounts he was quite suspicious of writing in general. (Somewhat ironically, Plato gives a written account of Socrates's criticism of writing as an impediment to thought and a poison for memory in *Phaedrus*.[3]) Everything we know about his life and thought comes second- and thirdhand in the writings of others; in *Memorabilia*, Socrates's companion Xenophon offered a chronical of his trial. The comic playwright Aristophanes famously lampooned Socrates in his play *The Clouds*. In all cases, he is portrayed as having no gainful employment, living off the benefaction of his admirers, walking the streets of Athens barefoot in a worn-out cloak, engaging anyone who would stop and listen in conversation. On the conventionality–weirdness continuum, Socrates definitely inclines toward the weird, though probably not as far out as the Cynics. However, we learn most about Socrates's ideas in the dialogues written by his student, Plato (c. 428–347 BCE). Nearly all of Plato's works are written in dialogue form (*Apology* is one of the few exceptions where Socrates holds the floor and dialogue with others is kept to a minimum), and Socrates is the protagonist of most of Plato's writings. So, when we talk about the philosophical position that we might call "Socratic," we are really talking about Platonism.

If we look deeper into Socrates's claims of ignorance in *Apology*, we discover a healthy dose of irony in the claim. (Irony is a pronounced feature of Socrates's personality as Plato presents him.) Socrates couches his claims of ignorance in a larger narrative arc that includes the story of his friend Chaerephon approaching the Temple of Delphi, which is dedicated to the god Apollo, to have revealed finally whether Socrates is indeed wise. Socrates recounts,

> [Chaerephon] asked whether there was anyone wiser than myself. The priestess replied that there was no one. . . . After puzzling about it for some time, I set myself at last with considerable reluctance to check the truth of it in the following way. I went to interview a man with a high reputation for wisdom, because I felt that here if anywhere I should succeed in disproving the oracle and pointing out to my divine authority, You said that I was the wisest of men, but here is a man who is wiser than I am.[4]

Alas, Socrates continues, his interview revealed that this man's reputation for wisdom was overblown (as was the man's confidence that his reputation was earned). Upon leaving this interview, Socrates concluded, "neither of us has any knowledge to boast of, but he thinks that he knows something which he does not know, whereas I am quite conscious of my ignorance. At any rate it seems I am wiser than he is to this small extent, that I do not think I know what I do not know."[5] Based on his further conversations with other "wise" men, Socrates concludes that genuine wisdom is a divine quality, ultimately beyond human attainment, in comparison with which human wisdom pales: "The wisest of you men is he who has realized, like Socrates, that in respect of wisdom he is really worthless."[6] We will return to this puzzling claim—that the wise person is wise because she knows she lacks wisdom—in the second part of this book.

It is important to point out, however, that there is a deep irony in nearly everything Socrates says; the dialogues are always stilted in his favor, and he always wins the conversation in the end, so we ought to have some suspicions about Socrates's claims of ignorance. There were, however, other philosophical schools, nearly contemporaneous with Plato's, that were rigorously unironic in their cultivation of ignorance; paramount among these sincere purveyors of ignorance were the Skeptics, sometimes called Pyrrhonists, or Pyrrhonian Skeptics, after the purported founder of the movement, Pyrrho (ca. 365–270 BCE). Like Socrates, Pyrrho left no writings behind, and accounts we have of his life and thought are sparse and fragmentary. Most of what we know about Skeptical thought and ideas comes from Sextus Empiricus, a physician who lived sometime during the second and third centuries CE.

The Skeptics, as their moniker suggests, were dubious that humans could ultimately know anything at all. Confident that equally valid pro and con arguments could be mounted for any opinion, they concluded that any opinion was as good as any other, thus, the attempt to defend any set of beliefs as superior was doomed to fail. Sextus explains the Skeptical principle as such:

> Men of talent, who were perturbed by the contradiction in things and in doubt as to which of the alternatives they ought to accept, were led on to inquire what is true in things and what false, hoping by the settlement of this question to attain quietude. The main Skeptic system is that of opposing to every

proposition an equal proposition; for we believe that as a consequence of this we end by ceasing to dogmatize.[7]

The Skeptics' ideal, then, was the suspension of all belief and, finally, the refusal to advance any opinions at all—other than the opinion that no opinions are better than any others—with the goal of quieting the mind. In other words, since fretting over apparent contradictions leads to mental unease, the Skeptical goal is to not fret: "'Suspense' is a state of mental rest owing to which we neither deny nor affirm anything."[8] In other words, try not to get too attached to your own ideas because they will likely turn out to be short-sighted or just plain wrong. Mental ease, the closest thing to happiness for the Skeptics, resides in weighing things with a grain of salt.

We might expect that such an extreme position on the emptiness of opinions might lead the Skeptics to engage in forms of behavior that would place them next to the Cynics on the conventionality–weirdness spectrum, but the opposite was the case. The Skeptics tended to be conformists, leading utterly conventional lives, though not because social conventions were any better than eccentricity. If no opinions are better than any others, if no beliefs are superior, then no way of life is any better than any other; conformity with social convention is just easier. Sextus explains, "We follow a line of reasoning which, in accordance with appearances, points us to a life conformable to the customs of our country and its laws and institutions, and to our own instinctive feelings."[9] This is not your run-of-the-mill conformism, but one that is reached through the cultivation of a philosophical way of life. In short, (systematic) ignorance is bliss.

One commentator has suggested that following through on the Pyrrhonian ideal of holding no beliefs at all becomes a kind of "cognitive suicide."[10] If one refuses to form any beliefs, she gives up any possibility of generating any motives to act, and hence, she risks giving up acting altogether: if I suspend my belief that eating is necessary for continued existence, then I may be inclined to stop eating; my cognitive suicide turns into actual, physical suicide. So, few modern philosophers have been willing to press Pyrrhonian

Skepticism to its extremes. However, one important modern figure offered a moderated version of Skepticism as a philosophical ideal, the Scottish philosopher, David Hume (1711–1776 CE).

Hume argued that all knowledge about the world is gained through perception. My commerce with the world takes place through my senses, thus my knowledge is formed entirely through the association of sense impressions and the logical inferences I draw from those impressions. Yet, as Hume pointed out, if I think about my experience of the world as the association of sense impressions, and my knowledge of the world as the inferences I draw from those sense impressions, then a gap opens up between experience and knowledge that cannot be filled by perception itself. Take, for instance, the inference of the existence of cause-and-effect: supposed someone witnesses a billiard ball rolling across the billiard table, striking another billiard ball, "causing" it to move (one of Hume's favored examples). The relation of causation is an inference he makes based on the association of sense impressions presented to him: rolling ball + contact + movement of second ball. In other words, he infers that the first ball has transferred its momentum to the second ball upon contact, causing the second ball to move. As Hume points out, however, he does not *see* the transfer of momentum, hence the inference of causation is not, strictly speaking, supported by the association of sense impressions: "He immediately infers the existence of one object from the appearance of another. Yet he has not, by all his experience, acquired any idea or knowledge of the secret power by which the one object produces the other; nor is it, by any process of reasoning, he is engaged to draw this inference."[11] Hume then asks what principle fills the gap between experience and inference; his response is that the inference is drawn not from reason, per se, but from *habit and custom*: "Custom . . . is the great guide of human life. It is that principle alone which renders our experience useful to us, and makes us expect, for the future, a similar train of events with those which have appeared in the past."[12] That is to say, we make our inferences about reality based on the *habit* of assuming that present and future events will follow the same course as relevantly similar past ones—assuming that there is some causal force behind similar events—and our articulation of that causal force is shaped by the *customs* of the place where we live. In other words, the greater part of our knowledge of the world rests on the shaky foundations of common sense and conventional wisdom, the very things the philosopher, and especially the Skeptical philosopher, places in question.

When pressed on whether such shaky foundations are sufficient to base philosophical understanding on, Hume argued that such common sense and conventional wisdom are all we have, in the end. However, rather than draw the hard-core Pyrrhonian conclusion that we should strive to hold no beliefs whatsoever, Hume defended a *mitigated* skepticism "which may be both durable and useful" for daily life, a kind of skepticism that would instill some humility about what we think we know:

> And if any of the learned be inclined, from their natural temper, to haughtiness and obstinacy, a small tincture of Pyrrhonism might abate their pride, by showing them that the few advantages which they have attained over their fellows, are but inconsiderable, if compared with the universal perplexity and confusion, which is inherent in human nature. In general, there is a degree of doubt, and caution, and modesty, which, in all kinds of scrutiny and decision, ought for ever to accompany a just reasoner.[13]

For Hume, as for Socrates, a cultivated sense of ignorance makes for a good philosopher.

WONDERING

With rare exceptions, however, the cultivation of a sense of ignorance is not the end in itself. Rather, coming to a sense of what we do not know kick starts a second intellectual virtue, a sense of curiosity or *wonder* about things. In Plato's dialogue *Theaetetus*, Socrates praises one of his interlocutors, Theaetetus, the namesake of the dialogue, for his sense of wonder: "This sense of wonder is the mark of the philosopher. Philosophy indeed has no other origin . . ."[14] *Theaetetus* is an interesting dialogue for our purposes, given that the central topic of the dialogue concerns the nature of knowledge, truth, and wisdom. As usual, Socrates claims to know nothing about knowledge and engages Theaetetus and his teacher Theodorus to explain what knowledge is. Theaetetus (and Theodorus) espouse an account of knowledge that corresponds to that of another Greek philosopher, Protagoras (ca. 490–420 BCE), who infamously claimed *that man is the measure of all things.* While it is difficult to determine what Protagoras meant by this claim—we only possess fragments of his writings—his contemporaries and critics generally understood it to mean something like *truth is in the eye of the beholder.*

The way Theaetetus interprets the Protagorean dictum is that knowledge is a matter of perception: "It seems to me that one who knows something is perceiving the thing he knows, and, so far as I can see at present, knowledge is nothing but perception."[15] This definition launches Socrates and his dialogue partners on a path of questions and answers that soon reveals the problematic nature of this account of knowledge. As Socrates argues throughout the dialogue, perception cannot be the ground of knowledge because individuals frequently perceive things differently and form differing, sometimes contradictory, opinions based on their differing perceptions. If we base our understanding of knowledge, truth, and wisdom on perception, then we are committed to the claim that everyone's account is as good as anyone else's, a claim that Socrates cannot countenance, and, it turns out, neither can Theaetetus when pressed on the issue. (We will return to the disconnect between knowledge and perception in the next chapter.)

The dialogue concludes with Socrates convincing Theaetetus that knowledge, whatever knowledge is, cannot be mere perception, but must rest on some firmer foundation. Notice, that Socrates and Theaetetus come no closer to determining what knowledge is, only what it is not, but that is not nothing, as Socrates explains:

HOW TO THINK PHILOSOPHICALLY

> Then supposing you should ever henceforth try to conceive
> afresh, Theaetetus, if you succeed, your embryo thoughts
> will be the better as a consequence of today's scrutiny,
> and if you remain barren, you will be gentler and more
> agreeable to your companions, having the good sense not
> to fancy you know what you do not know. For that, and no
> more, is all that my art can effect; nor have I any of that
> knowledge possessed by all the great and admirable men
> of our own day or of the past.[16]

The moral of the story: be clear about what you do not know, and
keep wondering until you come to know it.

Plato's pupil, Aristotle, makes clearer the connection between a
sense of ignorance and the attendant wonder that leads to the philosophical way of life. In *Metaphysics*, Aristotle equates philosophy with
a passion to know, a passion that is born out of a sense of ignorance
and an attendant wonder about the nature of things:

> For it is owing to their wonder that men both now begin and
> at first began to philosophize; they wondered originally at the
> obvious difficulties, then advanced little by little and stated
> difficulties about greater matters, e.g. about the phenomena of
> the moon and those of the sun and of the stars, and about the
> genesis of the universe. And a man who is puzzled and won-
> ders thinks himself ignorant (whence even the lover of myth
> is in a sense a lover of Wisdom; for the myth is composed of
> wonders); therefore since they philosophize in order to escape
> from ignorance, evidently they were pursuing science in order
> to know, and not for any utilitarian end.[17]

From the beginning, Aristotle argued, humans were driven to seek
knowledge about the nature of things, and that drive is grounded in
a sense of our own ignorance and a wonder about things, a way of life
that is, at bottom, philosophical. We are all, according to Aristotle,
philosophers to some degree.

POSTLUDE: SOME THOUGHTS REGARDING
HEDGEHOGS AND FOXES

In an influential essay entitled *The Hedgehog and the Fox*, the twentieth century historian and philosopher Isaiah Berlin (1909–1997) constructed a typology to categorize artists and intellectuals according to their primary orientation to ideas and to thinking about the world in general; as the title of the essay indicates, Berlin suggested that thinkers can be characterized broadly either as hedgehogs or foxes:

> For there exists a great chasm between those, on one side, who relate everything to a single central vision, one system less or more coherent or articulate, in terms of which they understand, think, and feel—a single, universal, organizing principle in terms of which alone all that they are and say has significance—and, on the other side, those who pursue many ends, often unrelated and even contradictory, connected, if at all, only in some *de facto* way . . . these last lead lives, perform acts, and entertain ideas that are centrifugal rather than centripetal, their thought is scattered or diffused, moving on many levels, seizing upon the essence of a vast variety of experiences and objects for what they are in themselves, without . . . seeking to fit them into, or exclude them from, any one unchanging, all-embracing . . . unitary inner vision. The first kind of intellectual and artistic personality belongs to the hedgehogs, the second to the foxes . . .[18]

In summary, hedgehogs focus on one big idea and organize all other ideas and experiences around and through that one big idea. Foxes on the other hand, are fascinated by things as they occur, look for some kind individual account of the thing in question—more or less independent of other accounts of other things—and then, just as often, move onto the next thing.

Berlin constructs his typology from a fragment by an ancient Greek poet, Archilochus, that reads, "The fox knows many things, but the hedgehog knows one big thing," and is generally interpreted to mean that, contrary to appearances, the advantage ultimately goes to the hedgehog. Berlin suspends judgment over whether the hedgehog or the fox is finally better off and instead presents the distinction as a useful, if only half serious, way to think about the different ways in which those who have taken up the life of the mind pursue their various subject matters. To be clear, Berlin's essay is not really about hedgehog-intellectuals and fox-intellectuals, but about novelist Leo Tolstoy's understanding of history (Berlin characterized Tolstoy as a fox who wants to be a hedgehog), but the distinction between hedgehogs and foxes is the aspect of the essay that has withstood the test of time and that has been redeployed to advance many different agendas. (So, I will unscrupulously follow this tradition of using Berlin's distinction to advance an idea that is only tangentially related to his own purposes.)

We might, without too much oversimplification, think of the philosophical form of life as issuing in two basic directions: the hedgehog-direction and the fox-direction. To be clear, hedgehogs are not more philosophical than foxes, nor is the opposite the case. Rather, the cultivation of a sense of ignorance and a sense of wonder about things can point people in different directions, and the direction chosen shapes the way philosophy plays out in action, and sometimes in surprising ways. For instance, Berlin characterizes Plato (the pupil of Socrates, who claims to know nothing) as an arch-hedgehog, and Aristotle (the pupil of Plato, the arch-hedgehog) as a classic example of a fox. While I do not want to press the distinction between hedgehogs and foxes too far—and I will not press it into service too rigorously in the rest of this book—I do find it a useful way to think about different ways of living and thinking philosophically.

Finally, I should fess up to my own fox nature if it is not apparent already. I do not argue that it is better to be a fox than a hedgehog; I am just wired that way. Most people who have had an opinion have argued the opposite, that it is better to be a hedgehog than a fox. (Most people who have opinions about hedgehogs and foxes are hedgehogs.) There is another version of the hedgehog–fox distinction in the ancient sources: a fable attributed to Aesop, the ancient Greek moralist, about the fox and the cat presents a remarkably similar idea. In the fable, the fox expresses his doubts that the cat knows as many tricks for escaping pursuers as the fox knows. As they are conversing, they hear hounds approaching; the cat immediately acts on its only trick and climbs a tree, thus evading capture. The fox, on the other hand, knowing so many different tricks, cannot decide where to start, tries a little of everything, and is finally captured. So, maybe it *is* better to be a hedgehog than a fox. Being a fox, I have no opinion.

NOTES

1 Pierre Hadot, *What is Ancient Philosophy?*, trans. Michael Chase (Cambridge, MA: Harvard University Press, 2002), 108–109.

2 Plato, "Apology," 20.e, in *Plato: Collected Dialogues*, ed. Edith Hamilton and Huntington Cairns, trans. Hugh Tredennick (Princeton, NJ: Princeton University Press, 1961), 7.

3 Plato, "Phaedrus," 274.d-275.b, in *Plato: Collected Dialogues*, ed. Edith Hamilton and Huntington Cairns, trans. R. Hackforth (Princeton, NJ: Princeton University Press, 1961), 520.

4 Plato, "Apology," 21.a, 21.c, 7.

5 Plato, "Apology," 21.d, 8.

6 Plato, "Apology," 23.b, 9.

7 Sextus Empiricus, *Outlines of Pyrrhonism*, trans. R. G. Bury (Cambridge, MA: Harvard University Press, 1933), I.12.

8 Sextus Empiricus, *Outlines of Pyrrhonism*, I.10.

9 Sextus Empiricus, *Outlines of Pyrrhonism*, I.17.

10 Katja Vogt, "Ancient Skepticism," *The Stanford Encyclopedia of Philosophy*, last modified, July 20, 2018, https://plato.stanford.edu/entries/skepticism-ancient/.

11 David Hume, "An Enquiry Concerning Human Understanding," in *Enquiries Concerning Human Understanding and Concerning the Principles of Morals,* 3rd ed. (New York: Oxford University Press, 1975), 42.

12 Hume, "An Enquiry Concerning Human Understanding," 44.

13 Hume, "An Enquiry Concerning Human Understanding," 161–62.

14 Plato, "Theaetetus," 155.d, in *Plato: Collected Dialogues*, ed. Edith Hamilton and Huntington Cairns, trans. Francis MacDonald Cornford (Princeton, NJ: Princeton University Press, 1961), 860.

15 Plato, "Theaetetus," 152.e, 857.

16 Plato, "Theaetetus," 210.c, 919.

17 Aristotle, "Metaphysics," 982b.11–22, in *The Basic Works of Aristotle*, ed.
    Richard McKeon, trans. W. D. Ross (New York: Random House, 1941), 692.

18 Isaiah Berlin, *The Hedgehog and the Fox: An Essay on Tolstoy's View of
    History* (New York: Simon and Schuster, 1953), 1–2.

CHAPTER THREE

Seeing Things as They Are

The Goal of the Philosophical Life

APPEARANCE AND REALITY

In book seven of *Republic*, generally recognized to be among his most important dialogues, Plato presents what is surely one of the most cited passages in the history of Western thought, the infamous cave allegory (see Figure 3.1). Generations of first year college students have been subjected to this passage and likely had to deal with it at some other point in their college careers. (I admit, I have subjected my fair share of students to it.) In the passage, Socrates, again the protagonist, asks his dialogue partner, Glaucon, to imagine the following scenario:

> Picture men dwelling in a sort of subterranean cavern with a long entrance open to the light on its entire width. Conceive them as having their legs and necks fettered from childhood, so that they remain in the same spot, able to look forward only, and prevented by the fetters from turning their heads. Picture the light from a fire burning higher up and at a distance behind them, and between the fire and the prisoners and above them a road along which a low wall has been built, as the exhibitors of puppet shows have partitions before the men themselves above which they show the puppets.[1]

Figure 3.1 Plato's cave allegory.

Source: Ian Suk, "Allegory of the Cave," in Ian Suk and Rafael J. Tamargo, "Neo-platonic Imagery by Michelangelo in Sistine Chapel's *Separation of Light from Darkness*," *Journal of Biocommunication*, 42, no.1 (2018), accessed July 8, 2022, https://journals.uic.edu/ojs/index.php/jbc/article/view/9331/7506

Socrates then asks Glaucon to imagine what understanding of the world these prisoners bound at the bottom of the cave would have. Obviously, Socrates continues, their only experience of the world, and of themselves in that world, would be the shadows cast on the wall of their prison, and all their conversations about that experience would, likewise, be limited to talk about shadows. Having knowledge only of the shades cast on the back wall of the cave, they would think those shades to be the totality of the world. In other words, the prisoners would mistake shadows for reality.

Socrates further unfolds his allegory, asking Glaucon to suppose what it would be like if one of these prisoners broke his bonds and was able to step back and observe his situation. He would recognize that what he took for reality was just the shadows cast by a puppet show.

Socrates asks Glaucon to imagine further that the newly released prisoner was dragged by force to the mouth of the cave to witness the world outside; "Do you not think that he would find it painful to be so haled along, and would chafe at it, and when he came out into the light, that his eyes would be filled with its beams so that he would not be able to see even one of the things that we call real?"[2] However, Socrates continues, with habituation he would come to know a sense of the reality outside of his prison, and would come to see his release as a blessing, not a burden. Socrates concludes his allegory by asking Glaucon to ponder what it would be like for the man to return to those still bound at the floor of the cave: "Now if he should be required to contend with these perpetual prisoners in 'evaluating' these shadows while his vision was still dim and before his eyes were accustomed to the dark . . . would he not provoke laughter, and would it not be said of him that he had returned from his journey aloft with his eyes ruined and that it was not worthwhile even to attempt the ascent?"[3]

There is a lot going on in this allegory, and it plays a pivotal role in Plato's corpus. Among other things, it lays out in schematic form Plato's understanding of the true nature of reality, his metaphysical picture of things. Plato has left a deep impression on Western thought—one of the reasons this passage is so often cited—and we will return to this image later to fill in what it says about Plato's account of reality. Our focus here is on what the allegory says about common human understandings and about the philosopher's role in questioning these common understandings. This image of the cave explains Socrates's understanding of most of human existence. We are prisoners bound to a world of mere appearances, mistaking shadows for deeper realities. Our conventional wisdom and common-sense notions of the way things are become the fetters that bind us to this world of appearances. In short, we are trapped in a world of illusions. The philosopher is one who has slipped the fetters and begun the journey out of the cave; she has glimpsed, if imperfectly, the true world outside the prison of illusions and has come to understand the shadows for what they are: mere appearances. However, the philosopher is a humanitarian; she does not want to keep her burgeoning wisdom to herself. She is driven to help others shed the bonds of illusion. She has to spill the beans about what she knows, often to an unreceptive audience.

The drive to question what everyone takes for granted is, as we have already discussed, what makes the philosopher such an odd duck. The fact that her audience is so often reticent to hear the truth also makes her more unpopular, and here it is important to highlight a key factor of human existence: often, we just do not want to know the truth. Our bondage to illusions is, in large part, a self-imposed imprisonment; we have attachments to our illusions and often do not want to give them up. It is not just a matter of revealing the truth, the philosopher also must overcome the natural resistance to knowing, both in herself and in her audience.

ILLUSION AND TRUTH

There are many sources of illusion and many reasons for our resistance to giving it up. In some cases, illusion is simply a factor of naivete. In other cases, attachment to illusion is a more systemic feature of human existence and, hence, more difficult to overcome. We have encountered already the problem of a naive reliance on our perceptions. David Hume alerted us to the gap that opens between perceptual experience and inferences drawn from that experience: our actual experiences infrequently, if ever, support our inferences, hence our knowledge rests on shaky foundations. Yet, even though he argued that our inferences are based on certain habits of thinking and the customs that govern our common existence, even Hume thought that, if we could get better at focusing on what we actually perceive and apply a healthy dose of skepticism to our customary modes of explanation, our inferences could get better, that is, more logical. Indeed, Hume was deeply critical of some aspects of the conventional wisdom of his times, in particular the tendency to rely on notions of God and divine will as causal explanations. (Hume's dismissal of the miracles as explanatory inferences is legendary and, for many, decisive;

if we press further, he argued, we will likely find better, "non-supernatural" explanations.[4])

Before Hume, the French philosopher and scientist René Descartes (1596–1650 CE) pressed this skepticism about our perceptual experience to its extreme. Descartes begins his *Meditations on First Philosophy* with an admission of his previous naivete about the nature of reality and his commitment to overcome this credulity:

> Several years have now passed since I first realized how numerous were the false opinions that in my youth I had taken to be true, and thus how doubtful were all those that I had subsequently built upon them. And I realized that once in my life I had to raze everything to the ground and begin again from the original foundations, if I wanted to establish anything firm and lasting in the sciences.... At last I will apply myself earnestly an unreservedly to this demolition of my opinions.[5]

Thus begins Descartes's journey to establish firm foundations upon which to establish an indubitable understanding of the nature of reality.

Descartes itemizes the various things that can be doubted in the search for those things that cannot. First, on the chopping block of things that are dubitable is the information provided by our senses. While we suffer from the tendency to rely on our senses for understanding the world, those senses frequently give us faulty information—our eyes can be tricked by optical illusions, colors appear differently in different lighting conditions, sleight-of-hand artists can make it appear that they produce coins out of thin air, and so on. Our senses, Descartes suggests, cannot be trusted. And, if there is any last corner where we might be inclined to grant legitimacy to our senses, Descartes lays waste to any final trust in our perceptions by pointing out our dreaming states: "As I consider these matters more carefully, I see plainly that there are no definite signs by which to distinguish being awake from being asleep."[6] Even the line between dreaming and waking life is dubious.

He concludes by placing in suspicion the one customary opinion that would have provided some sense of certainty for someone
in his situation, the existence of divine providence. Descartes was
educated by Roman Catholic Jesuits, so would have been taught that
the existence of a benevolent deity was indubitable, but he goes so far
as to turn his meditation in the opposite direction: "I will suppose
not a supremely good God . . . but rather an evil genius, supremely
powerful and clever, who has directed his entire effort at deceiving
me. . . . I will remain resolute and steadfast in this meditation . . .
to withhold my assent to what is false, lest this deceiver, however
powerful, however clever he may be, have any effect on me."[7] To
be clear, in the meditations, Descartes is engaged in what philosophers call a "thought experiment;" he does not really suppose the
existence of an evil genius, but uses this idea to see how far doubt
can be pressed. And, indeed, the thought that my sense of reality is
a vast illusion created by a being intent on deceiving me leaves little
foundation on which to ground understanding. I cannot trust my
senses; indeed, I cannot even trust that I have any senses. The whole
of reality—including myself—seems to evaporate in a dizzying abyss
of doubt. Yet, even amid this hyperbolic doubt, Descartes discovers
one indubitable fact: "What about thinking? Here I make my dis-
covery: thought exists; it alone cannot be separated from me. I am;
I exist—this is certain. . . . I am a true thing and I am truly existing;
but what kind of thing? I have said it already: a thinking thing."[8] No
matter how much I doubt, one indubitable thing dawns: *cogito ergo
sum*, I think, therefore I am.

Thus, Descartes asserts, *reason*, not sense perception, brings me
to the one indubitable foundation, *the existence of (my) mind*, upon
which to rebuild an understanding of the world. However, it is difficult to discern how to make the move from the certainty that I
exist to any certainty that anything else does: How do I know that
I am not a disembodied mind or, a more contemporary variation,
a brain in a vat artificially being fed electro-chemical stimuli by an
evil genius? Descartes thought he had made his way back from the
mind to reality—which involved reclaiming one of the things he

earlier placed in doubt: the existence of a benevolent deity—but few have been convinced by his argument. Hume thought Descartes ridiculous; the certainty of my own existence may be as useless as it is indubitable for getting me any trenchant understanding of reality. A later philosopher, Immanuel Kant, offered perhaps a better understanding of the disconnect between the senses and reality, and the way reason can help us think our way past the apparent impasse.

Kant (1724–1804 CE) shared with Descartes a mistrust of our senses as a ground for understanding, and he shared with Hume the recognition that our inferences about reality are not supported by sense perceptions. Yet, he found Descartes's attempt to get from mind to reality implausible and Hume's concessions to habit and custom problematic. He hoped to locate a critical use of reason that could give some firm footing to understanding. Kant puts it this way:

> If the senses merely represent something to us **as it appears**, then this something must also be in itself a thing, and an object of non-sensible intuition, i.e., of the understanding, i.e., a cognition must be possible in which no sensibility is encountered, and which alone has absolutely objective reality, through which, namely, objects are represented to us **as they are**, in contrast to the empirical use of our understanding, in which things are only cognized **as they appear**.[9]

If this sentence is not clear to you, do not despair; Kant is famous for long, convoluted expressions that are difficult to decipher and, perhaps, impossible to fully understand (ironic, since he aimed to explain what it means to understand). Put simply, Kant conjoins two, for him absolute and opposed, distinctions: perception versus understanding, and things as they appear versus things as they are *in themselves*. Like Hume, Kant asserts that our commerce with the world comes through perception and yields a stream of sense impressions about which we can make inferences. These inferences are not genuine understanding for Kant, however, because they are purely subjective. My perceptions are purely mine: you view the world from your location, and I view it from mine; even if you could occupy my location, things would look different because of differences in our perceptual make up. Like Descartes, Kant asserts that perceptions are deceptive and cannot deliver objective, universally valid understanding of the things *in themselves*.

So, it appears that we are at an impasse: our experience of the world is of *things as they appear* (*phaenomena*, literally "appearances"), but we can have no idea whether the appearances correspond, in any universally valid way, to the *things in themselves*. Perhaps we are consigned to habit and custom or the disconcerting possibility that we are brains in vats. But reason comes to our aid precisely here: while reason can never lead us to a full understanding of the reality behind appearances, as Descartes seemed to think it could, reason can perform a critical function of recognizing what it cannot do and what it cannot know, and in that sense, reason thinks itself past its own limitations. In other words, by reasoning through things, I can recognize the difference between things as they appear and things in themselves, understand that my experience is limited to things as they appear, and reach through to the necessary conditions for having any experience whatsoever; that is to say, I can form an understanding, prior to any particular experience, of what is required to have that experience. Thus, Kant suggests, I can know that there are things out there, that things exist in space and time and are subject to cause and effect, and so on, because without these factors there would be no experience at all. In short, though I can never be sure that my experience of things corresponds to the way things are, I can know that the world must be a certain way in order for me to have experiences, and that is not nothing.

We have gotten into the weeds with Descartes and Kant. Suffice it to say, that philosophers, by and large, are suspicious of the uncritical acceptance of our perceptions. The goal is to dig beneath the surface of common sense in search of deeper understanding. However, one aspect of our existence frequently gets in the way of our attempts to get behind our perceptions to find those deeper understandings: our appetitive nature. By appetite, we are speaking of a broader reality that mere hunger and need for sustenance. While appetite includes the impulse toward physical needs, it also points to the broader reality of passion and desire generally. Our appetitive nature can cloud our reasoning. As we all know, when strong passions and desires overtake us, they disarm our faculties. (The Latin root of the word passion, *passio*, is the same as that for passivity and for suffering. In that sense, our reasoning is passive in the face of overwhelming desires; thinking suffers the slings of the passions!)

One of the most important philosophers in the Christian tradition, St. Augustine of Hippo (354–430 CE), made the exposition of the corrupting influence of our appetites a major aspect of his thinking. Importantly, however, for Augustine, our passions and desires are not corrupting in and of themselves; they become so when we allow them to divert us from some higher purpose. Short of this act of will, whereby we give ourselves over to our appetites, passion and desire are good, indeed necessary for our survival and happiness. Augustine explains, "All things are good; better in proportion as they are better measured, formed and ordered, less good where there is less of measure, form and order. These three things, measure, form and order . . . are as it were generic good things to be found in all that God has created, whether spirit or body."[10] Thus, so long as desires and passions remain measured and ordered, they are good and serve their own proper aims; when we allow them to depart from that measure and order they become a source of evil—for Augustine, sin or the turning away from the supreme good, the will of God. Sin is a corruption of an otherwise good—measured, formed, and ordered—nature.

In this sense, there is no problem with passion and desire, per se, rather the problem lies in the way our nature can become corrupted in letting passion and desire run away with us. Augustine concludes, "When reason rules these emotions, a man must be said to be well ordered. There is no right order, indeed there is no order at all, where the better is subordinated to the worse."[11] Here, then, is the rub—and philosophers generally agree with Augustine on this point: the corruption lies not in the appetites themselves but in some other region of our nature or soul related to appetite; that region is our will. There are two sources of direction for the will: reason and appetite. So long as reason directs the will, our soul maintains its measure, order, and form; when our will becomes unmoored from reason in such a way that the appetite comes to rule, then disorder and corruption set in. Thus, sin and evil are not so much a species of action as a disease within the soul that clouds our sense of reality and disables our capacity to act in accord with that reality. Augustine went on to argue that once corruption has manifested itself—a corruption made almost inevitable by original sin—the will is unable to extricate itself from its disordered state and must await the assistance of divine grace. This final move makes him a bit of an outlier in the broader tradition of Western philosophy (though it also makes him one of the principal figures in the formation of orthodox Christian theology). By and large, philosophers have argued that it is our responsibility not to let our emotions run away with us, and our responsibility to rectify the situation when they do.

So, one important factor that keeps us fettered to our illusions is an internal one, that is, a corruption of our internal state of understanding and willing. There are other fetters external to us, however, namely our distractions with the everyday and the common opinions of those we interact with. The twentieth-century philosopher Martin Heidegger (1889–1976 CE) dubbed this distraction with the everyday *fallenness*. In this state of fallenness, *Dasein*—"being-there," the German term Heidegger used to signify human being—becomes absorbed into or swallowed up by "the *they*"—Heidegger's terminology for conventional opinion or common sense. He explains this state of fallenness as such:

> This "absorption in . . ." has mostly the character of Being-lost in the publicness of the 'they'. Dasein has, in the first instance, fallen away from itself as an authentic potentiality for Being its Self, and has fallen into the 'world'. 'Fallenness' into the 'world' means an absorption in Being-with-one-another, in so far as the latter is guided by idle talk, curiosity, and ambiguity.[12]

Heidegger invents his own terminology, which often makes relatively simple ideas more complicated, and this tendency is on display in this short passage. (Heidegger has reasons for this invention of terminology, but we need not go into them here.) Put simply, what he means is that humans tend to get caught up in common opinion—idle talk, curiosity, and ambiguous formulations of reality—in such a way that they lose track of their concerns to know the truth about things and live a certain kind of life. *Dasein* falls into the world in such a way that it becomes distracted by commonsensical notions that *they* talk about and loses track of its own, authentic concerns. Such a life is synonymous with the life of Socrates's captives in the allegory of the cave. *Dasein* can only reconstitute itself as an authentic self— as true understanding of reality and effective agency—by tearing itself away from its captivity to idle talk, curiosity, and ambiguous understandings.

As Socrates indicates in *Republic*, however, this effort to extricate ourselves from the bondage of common opinion is difficult because we find some comfort in the opinions of the crowd. We often fall into the habit of assuming that consensus lends credibility to opinions, or even that the majority opinion is the safe bet. Philosophers question this assumption. Danish philosopher Søren Kierkegaard (1813–1855 CE) puts the matter in its most extreme form:

> There is a view of life that holds that truth is where the crowd is, that truth itself needs to have the crowd on its side. There is another view of life that holds that wherever the crowd is, untruth is, so that even if—to carry the matter to its ultimate for a moment—all individuals who, separately, secretly possessed the truth were to come together in a crowd (in such a way, however, that 'the crowd' acquired any *deciding*, voting, noisy, loud significance), untruth would promptly be present there.[13]

Imagine, Kierkegaard suggests, that one knows something in private, but then somehow relied on the agreement of others to determine for himself the truth of that thing. Somehow, the reliance on others' judgments and opinions would make the truth a kind of untruth.

Kierkegaard was a great lover of absurdity and loved to employ ironic formulations to push issues to their furthest logical (and absurd) conclusions, so we should take his statements about truth and untruth with a grain of salt.[14] There is, nonetheless, a grain of philosophical truth in these statements about untruth that is worth exploring. We might put it this way: If something is true, it is true whether the majority thinks so or not, indeed, whether anybody thinks so or not. Philosophers want to figure out what is true, not what people think is true. And this means that going along with the crowd, being absorbed into the *they*, uncritically accepting the dictates of conventional wisdom, even if the crowd, the *they*, or conventional wisdom turn out to be right, runs against the philosophical grain. Or, perhaps better stated, the philosophical life runs against the grain of common sense.

If it seems that philosophers are constitutionally contentious, that they question commonly held opinions on principle, that they are sometimes intent on pushing things to their most extreme conclusions . . . well, that is just what it means to live philosophically. Does this mean that philosophers are willing to entertain and adopt any absurd proposition that seems to run counter to popular opinion? To be more concrete about it, is somebody who subscribes to conspiracies about secret cabals within the government intent on tracking our every move and undermining our rights and freedoms *in the absence of any evidence whatsoever*, who denies the results of a democratic election *even in the face of clear evidence that the process was fair and free of corruption*, living a philosophical life? It may seem so at times; Kierkegaard, for one, often seems to suggest that the more absurd a proposition is, the more passionately one should subscribe to it (see note 14 at the end of the chapter), but I suggest that this is a misreading.

The philosophical life is not about denying facts, dismissing evidence, or adopting absurd propositions. Living philosophically involves sorting out what the facts are, interpreting what the evidence means, and determining whether beliefs and opinions hold up under scrutiny. And this is because the philosopher has a stake in the truth. She does not just want to know it; she wants to live it. The ultimate end of the philosophical life is to live well, and to live well one must have a clear sense of how things really are.

POSTLUDE: A REFLECTION ON
BLUE PILLS AND RED PILLS

One of the exercises I do with students in my philosophy classes asks them to consider the following scenario:

> You are living a perfectly nice life: you have a successful job you love, a happy family, and many good friends. One day a mysterious figure named Agent Smith comes to you and reveals that you are living in a simulation. He explains that machines have taken over the world and put all humans in a simulation in order to use their bodies as batteries to keep the machines going. Each human inhabits their own simulation and no simulations are interlinked; everything that happens in the simulation is generated by the simulation itself. As individuals die their bodies are liquified to provide nutrients for the others; new bodies are produced through artificial insemination and then plugged into a simulation where they live out their lives as batteries for the machines.

Many readers will recognize that I am repurposing (with some professorial license) the basic theme of (what used to be) a very popular movie, *The Matrix*. In the film, the protagonist, a computer programmer/hacker named Thomas Anderson, a.k.a. Neo, suffers from nagging thoughts that there is more to reality than meets the eye. In his search to discover this truth beneath appearances, he encounters an infamous computer hacker, Morpheus, who presents Neo with a choice: he can take a blue pill, return to his mundane existence, no questions asked, or take a red pill and have the truth about reality revealed to him. Happily for the movie-goers, Neo chooses the red pill, and we are off to the battle between the humans and their robot overlords.[15]

Besides being a thoroughly enjoyable film, which I highly recommend if you have not seen it, *The Matrix* raises a number of very interesting questions, indeed precisely the kinds of questions we have been dealing with in this chapter. In the film, human beings are literally prisoners who from birth are fed images by mechanical puppeteers. They are literally brains in vats, or rather brains in bodies in vats, being artificially fed electrochemical stimuli by evil robotic geniuses. And a few succeed in breaking free of their fetters and from the opinions of the crowd to find the truth beneath the illusion, in this case a diabolical truth and a manipulative illusion.

The ultimate question I ask students to consider is this one: "Agent Smith gives you the choice to leave the simulation, return to your embodied existence, and learn the truth about reality, or to remain in the simulation, continue to have your body used as a battery, and have the revelation removed from your memory. Which should you choose, and why should you choose it?" In short, I ask students whether they should remain in their happy, if artificial, life, or face the truth, even if it is largely unknown and possibly dangerous. A fair number of my students (more than I am comfortable with) argue vehemently that the correct choice is to stay in the illusion, that if you do not know you are a slave being used as a battery then it is not so bad. Happily, for me, however, the majority just find something wrong about living in an illusion, especially if living the illusion entails having no genuine control over your life.

Who knows what choice they would make if actually faced with this bizarre situation; I hope I would take the red pill, but I can't know for sure. My hope is that I and my students would act like philosophers.

NOTES

1 Plato, "Republic," 514.a-b, in *Plato: Collected Dialogues*, ed. Edith Hamilton and Huntington Cairns, trans. Paul Shorey (Princeton, NJ: Princeton University Press, 1961), 747.

2 Plato, "Republic," 516.a, 748.

3 Plato, "Republic," 517.a, 749.

4 David Hume, "An Enquiry Concerning Human Understanding," in *Enquiries Concerning Human Understanding and Concerning the Principles of Morals*, 3rd ed. (New York: Oxford University Press, 1975), 74–90.

5 René Descartes, "Meditations on First Philosophy," in *Discourse on Method and Meditations on First Philosophy*, 3rd ed., trans. Donald A. Cress (Indianapolis: Hackett, 1993), 59.

6 Descartes, "Meditations on First Philosophy," 60.

7 Descartes, "Meditations on First Philosophy," 62–63.

8 Descartes, "Meditations on First Philosophy," 65.

9 Immanuel Kant, *Critique of Pure Reason*, trans. and ed. Paul Guyer and Allen W. Wood (Cambridge: Cambridge University Press, 1998), 347.

10 Augustine, "The Nature of the Good Against the Manichees," in *The Library of Christian Classics: Augustine: Earlier Writings*, ed. and trans. John H. S. Burleigh (Philadelphia: Westminster Press, 1953), 327.

11 Augustine, "On Free Will," in Burleigh, ed., *The Library of Christian Classics*, 123.

12 Martin Heidegger, *Being and Time*, trans. John Macquarrie and Edward Robinson (San Francisco: Harper Collins, 1962), 220.

13 Søren Kierkegaard, *The Point of View on My Work as an Author*, ed. and trans. Howard V. Hong and Edna H. Hong (Princeton, NJ: Princeton University Press, 1998), 106.

14 In another work, Kierkegaard suggests that there are two ways to approach the question of truth: objectively and subjectively:

> When the question about truth is asked objectively, truth is reflected upon objectively as an object to which the knower relates himself. What is reflected upon is not the relation but that what he relates himself to is the truth, the true. If only that to which he relates himself to is the truth, the true, then the subject is in the truth. When the question about truth is asked subjectively, the individual's relation is reflected upon subjectively. If only the how of this relation is in truth, the individual is in truth, even if he in this way were to relate himself to untruth. (Kierkegaard, *Concluding Unscientific Postscript to Philosophical Fragments*, 199)

What Kierkegaard points to in this passage is the existential stake one has in her relation to what she holds to be true. To relate oneself *objectively* to a truth is to hold that truth at a distance such that the concern is whether that truth is actually (objectively) true. To relate oneself *subjectively* to a truth is to make that truth the center of one's life, to base one's existence on the conviction that it is true. Kierkegaard held that all existentially important truths were objectively uncertain, and hence one could only "be in the truth" existentially by relating oneself subjectively (and passionately) to those truths; existentially speaking, the truth is a matter of faith. Kierkegaard's own faith commitments were Christian, and he was greatly concerned with modern attempts to make Christianity "rational," that is, to provide objective foundations for Christian propositions. Such attempts, he argued, inevitably undermine and hollow out the fundamentally important assertions of Christianity, namely, that God became human, took upon Godself the sins of humanity, and died for the forgiveness of those sins. Kierkegaard asserted that these Christian truths are inextricably objectively uncertain, indeed, they are absurd; thus, there is no possible objective relation to them. Being a Christian entails passionately relating oneself to these truths in such a way that one's existence depends on their truth. For those of us who are not Christians, Kierkegaard's own faith commitments may not be so compelling. However, for some of us, his account of the existential importance of the things we hold to be true is.

15 *The Matrix*, written and directed by Lana Wachowski and Lilly Wachowski (Burbank, CA: Warner Bros., 1999).

CHAPTER FOUR

Attuning to the Way Things Are

The End of the Philosophical Life

Thus far, I have characterized the *form* of the philosophical life as asking the right kinds of questions with the *goal* of discovering the way things really are beneath the surface of appearances. Philosophers, however, have rarely been satisfied to stop here. For the most part, the philosophical endeavor is not a search for knowledge for its own sake. Rather, philosophical exploration is undertaken for the further *end* of learning how to live, at least in its historical foundations. Though modern and contemporary philosophical practice groups questions of how we should live into a specialized subdiscipline called ethics, even contemporary philosophers usually think that the end of all philosophizing somehow has something to do with learning how to live well. The purpose of this chapter is to hash out what a good life might look like from a philosophical point of view. I will approach the question of living well in four steps: the nature of happiness, how to deal with misfortune, Epicurean and Stoic views of the philosophical life, and the end of living well in situations of systemic injustice.

Typically, philosophers have associated living well with happiness: living well involves seeking the things that make for happiness.

Being happy translates into flourishing as a human being, so we will need to start by examining what happiness is. While philosophers and non-philosophers alike generally agree that happiness is what humans seek, they also recognize that happiness is difficult to find and difficult to keep once it is attained. Part of the reason for this is that life is full of misfortunes that interfere with our ability to find and maintain happiness. The next step, therefore, is to address the experience of fortunate and unfortunate events and the attendant ways of making sense of good and evil as they enter into a life; in large measure, we might view the philosophical project of living well as the cultivation of a set of practices designed to help us confront bad things that happen, to help us maintain happiness in the face of perceived misfortunes.

Again, while philosophers agree that living well involves happiness despite the inevitable misfortunes that arise in a lifetime, there is substantial disagreement about how to maintain happiness and confront misfortune. Thus, it will be worthwhile to compare two philosophical schools that competed directly with each other: Epicureanism and Stoicism. These two philosophical doctrines were among the most popular and most widespread in the Greek and Roman contexts, and both have had a profound influence on modern philosophy. Interestingly, Epicureans and Stoics agree on almost nothing except the nature of happiness, that is, that happiness ultimately rests in maintaining tranquility of mind and body.

I will conclude this exploration of the good life by introducing some modern problems into the mix, namely, how to address structural injustices that make it difficult, sometimes nearly impossible, for some individuals to seek, let alone secure, a good life. I will suggest that the final test of any philosophy worth advocating is to provide some sort of analysis and possible remedy for such structural injustices. In other words, living well involves not just securing one's own happiness, but in creating social environments that allow others, all others, to seek and secure theirs as well.

HAPPINESS AND HUMAN FLOURISHING

Philosophers and non-philosophers are in general agreement that a good life is characterized by happiness. But what exactly is happiness? Philosophers often operate out of a different understanding of happiness than we commonly do. We tend to think of happiness as a particular kind of emotion. We either feel happy or we do not feel happy, and there is not much we can do to control that feeling. We can put ourselves in situations that are likely to make us happy and avoid situations that make us unhappy, but whether we are or are not happy is largely beyond our control.

The Greek and Roman philosophers had a very different understanding of happiness and our ability to affect our own happiness. Happiness, on this view, has less to do with emotion and more to do with well-being. Aristotle, for example, characterizes happiness as a kind of activity. Recall that Aristotle argued that whatever it is that secures happiness, that thing must be *final*—be sought for itself alone—and *self-sufficient*—must, by itself, secure happiness without the aid of anything else. In Aristotle's understanding, happiness, or *eudaimonia*, resides in the activity of seeking those things that are capable of securing happiness. Remember that he thought that the cultivation of virtue was the only thing that would foot the bill; virtue is the only thing that is final and self-sufficient. Thus, characterizing happiness as the "chief good" in a human life, Aristotle concludes, "human good turns out to be activity of the soul in accordance with virtue, and if there are more than one virtue, in accordance with the best and most complete."[1]

It is not immediately clear what Aristotle means by an "activity of the soul," but the easiest way to make sense of the ancient understanding is to compare *happiness as a feeling* with *happiness as a disposition*. If happiness is a species of emotion, a feeling we are affected by, then we have little control over our own happiness. Feelings come and go, and our happiness is dependent on the whims of circumstance. I cannot control my happiness; the best I can do is try to engineer situations that are likely to make me happy and avoid situations that are likely to make me unhappy. Aristotle and other philosophers suggest that happiness is otherwise, that we have a great deal of control over our happiness regardless of circumstance.

Aristotle and others bank on the idea that humans can be dispositionally happy or unhappy. Dispositionally happy people can maintain their happiness despite circumstance. In other words, one who is genuinely happy chooses to be happy regardless of the situation she finds herself in. Becoming genuinely happy involves cultivating the right kinds of habits and the right kinds of mindsets that allow one to be happy and, as such, to flourish in whatever circumstance. Aristotle called these habits and mindsets—a.k.a., dispositions— virtues. The virtuous person has developed a certain way of looking at circumstances and habituated a certain way of acting in those circumstances; these dispositions buttress happiness and allow one to flourish whatever life brings. Thus, happiness is not so much a feeling as a choice of how one should live. The happy individual is one who has cultivated the dispositions that make for human flourishing.

Does a genuinely happy person no longer experience circumstances inimical to happiness? Is she immune to misfortunes? In the most general sense, no. Everyone encounters adversity in life, and that adversity presents a hinderance to our happiness. This is just a fact of life. In another sense, however, the dispositionally happy person has cultivated a way of seeing, understanding, and dealing with misfortune that takes some of the sting out of it. She has the ability to confront adversities in such a way that they do not destroy happiness, even when they present obstacles to flourishing. The value of a philosophical viewpoint, so the philosopher argues, is its ability to make sense of misfortune.

FORTUNE AND MISFORTUNE

Every life is affected by adversity. In many cases, adversities are comparatively minor—the loss of a prized possession, dissolution of an important relationship, and so on. In others, adversity is severe and devastating, for example, the death of loved one. Even in the luckiest life, one untouched by general misfortune, if such is imaginable, there exists the looming inevitability of one's own eventual demise. Death is the one absolute, indubitable destiny of every individual, whether he chooses to grapple with that destiny or not. A philosophy cannot protect one from adversity and misfortune; it is not some talisman that wards off evils. However, most philosophies have presented themselves as ways of life that, if adopted and practiced correctly, can take some of the sting out of the bad things that arise in a life.

One way to gauge the success or failure of a philosophical perspective is by its ability to provide a way to make sense of various ways fortune affects our lives. More to the point, a good philosophy articulates a general account of the nature of things that can explain why things happen the way they do. Let's flesh this out with a possible scenario: Suppose I am preparing a nice roast chicken and realize that I am out of lemons and rosemary, the two important ingredients that will make it just right; I hop in my car to run to the grocery, turn the key, and nothing—the motor refuses to turn over and start. There are a number of ways I might interpret this situation. I might think to myself: "The universe is a cruel place that constantly smashes people's happiness. Events have colluded to prevent me from making my roast chicken exactly the way it should be. Woe is me!" Most philosophers (and probably non-philosophers) would suggest that I am operating out of a defective philosophy, here. This is, quite simply, an absurd way to interpret the situation. I am embarrassed to say that I have interpreted similar situations in similar ways, knowing while I was doing so that such interpretations are absurd. (I have an automobile that is getting along in age, so I am practiced in interpreting situations like this one.)

The truth is, it is hard to fight the tendency to place ourselves, our projects, and our desires at the center of reality and to interpret aids and impediments as somehow geared toward the accomplishment or hinderance of those projects and desires. If doing so sounds absurd in the scenario of minor misfortune recounted above, it can seem less so in situations of catastrophic misfortune, for instance, life threatening illness or the untimely death of a loved one. Such catastrophic situations give misfortune the cast of *evil* and suggest, perhaps, that there is something fundamentally wrong with reality. A functioning philosophy, however, offers a broader account of reality that includes a compelling account of why such events happen. Aristotle, for example, argued that everything happens under the ineluctable influence of cause and effect.[2] Within such a framework, if one hangs onto an old car, he should expect that something will go wrong with it from time to time, and the car will not function. More significantly, disease and death are part of the broader scope of life, not vendettas reality exacts on individuals.

Now, explanation of the *how* of reality and *why* of misfortune is not the only thing a good philosophy offers. In addition, an effective philosophy helps explain the significance of misfortune relative to the individual and provides techniques to take the sting out of adversity. For example, the two philosophical positions we will spend time with next, Epicureanism and Stoicism, ask the individual to consider those things over which she has control and those things over which she does not have control in any situation she finds herself, particularly in situations of adversity. Returning to the scenario above, I have no control over whether my car starts, I only have control over how I respond to the fact that it will not. And here, I have a great number of choices, short- and long-term, that will take the sting out of adversity. I can call a friend for a ride to the grocery; I can make a less-than-perfect roast chicken, or even something otherwise; more long-term I can replace my car with something more reliable. (The same is the case with the more serious situations of illness—I can obey the doctor's orders in hopes of recovery—and the death of loved ones—I can fondly remember them and be grateful they were a part of my life.) Such reorientation not only takes the sting out of the situation, but it puts me back in charge by revealing what depends on me.

Interestingly, though the Epicureans and the Stoics both urge the individual to focus on what is in her power and provide techniques to aid in doing so, the techniques they offer are nearly diametrically opposed to each other, as are their accounts of the nature of reality and the place of misfortune within it.

EPICUREANS AND STOICS

Epicureanism and Stoicism were two of the four major philosophical schools, along with Platonism and Aristotelianism, in the Hellenistic period, that period of Greek cultural influence extending from the fourth century to the first century BCE. These two philosophical perspectives were direct competitors, and they exercised a huge influence on the surrounding civilization throughout the Hellenistic period and into the Imperial Roman context—roughly the first three centuries of the Common Era. The two schools offered similar accounts of human nature and similar understandings of happiness: the maintenance of tranquility in all situations. However, their accounts of the nature of reality (and the place of the human in that reality) and their understandings of how to maintain tranquility could not be farther apart. These facts make a comparison of Epicureanism and Stoicism an ideal way to explore how the choice of a philosophy entailed not just a particular way of thinking about things, but the adoption of a particular way of life. I will map this comparison in three stages: (1) a brief historical sketch of the emergence and influence of the two schools; (2) their differing understandings of the universe and the position of the human in that universe; and (3) their differing counsel on the nature of happiness, along with the unique philosophical practices geared at securing it.

The Emergence and Influence of Epicureanism and Stoicism

Epicureanism and Stoicism appeared, nearly contemporaneously, in the vicinity of Athens, Greece, near the end of the fourth century BCE. Both developed under the influence of founding figures and quickly organized into philosophical communities that espoused guiding sets of doctrines, instituted distinct pedagogical practices, and advocated the cultivation of unique ways of living. Epicureanism and Stoicism remained extremely influential into the Roman Imperial era, each undergoing a distinct development in the Latin context. Their influence declined after the fourth century CE when the Emperor Constantine the Great declared Christianity the favored philosophy of the Empire in 306 CE. By the end of the fourth century CE, Christianity became the official philosophy or religion of the Empire, squeezing out its primary competitors—Platonism, Aristotelianism, Epicureanism, and Stoicism—though these four would continue to exercise a major influence on the development of Christianity itself for at least the next millennium.

The Epicurean school developed around the ideas of its eponymous founder, Epicurus of Samos (ca. 342–270 BCE). In 306, Epicurus founded a philosophical community called the Garden. Professor of Philosophy Emily Austin describes the life and activities of the Garden:

> Epicurus and his fellow Epicureans lived at the Garden in private households, often with their spouses and children. They had a very active community life and spent much of their time talking, eating, drinking, and socializing together. . . . Uncharacteristically for his time, Epicurus welcomed women, slaves, and the poor to live, study, and write at the Garden. . . . Epicurus ran the school until his death of kidney stones in 270, at the age of seventy-two. The Garden remained active under Epicurean leadership until at least the late 50s BCE.[3]

Epicurus's influence continued into the later Roman Hellenistic and Imperial periods through the work of Philodemus of Gadara (ca. 110–35 BCE), Titus Lucretius Carus (a.k.a., Lucretius, ca. 94–50 BCE), and Diogenes of Oenoada (second century CE).

Stoicism emerged around the same time as Epicureanism, developing around the ideas of its two principal founders, Zeno of Citium

(333–261 BCE) and Chrysippus (282–206 BCE). Zeno was originally attracted to philosophy by the Cynic philosopher Crates. Recall that the Cynics represented the lunatic fringe of the Ancient Greek world; Zeno soon adopted a less extreme version of Cynic asceticism, thus launching a new philosophical worldview. Philosopher William Irvine explains that from its beginnings, "Zeno's school of philosophy enjoyed immediate success. His followers were initially called Zenonians, but because he was in the habit of giving his lectures from the Stoa Poikile [the portico of the Agora in Athens], they subsequently became known as the Stoics. . . ."[4] None of the writings of these founding figures of Stoicism survive (unlike Epicurus, from whom we have several letters and collections of sayings). Most of what we know of their life and thought comes from the historian Diogenes Laertius (ca. third century CE). The most significant extant works of the Stoic school come from the later Roman Imperial period. Unlike the Epicureans who generally formed tight knit communities that lived together and avoided public political activity on principle, the Stoics were active in the public political life of their cities. Indeed, two of the most important Roman Stoics were statesmen: Lucius Annaeus Seneca (a.k.a., Seneca the Younger, ca. 4–65 CE) served in the court of two Roman Emperors, and Marcus Aurelius (121–180 CE) was himself one of the most respected and admired Roman Emperors. For Seneca and Marcus Aurelius, along with the two other important Roman Stoics, Gaius Musonius Rufus (a.k.a., Musonius, ca. 20–100 CE) and Epictetus (ca. 50–135 CE), participation in public life was not only permissible, but represented something of a Stoic duty.

As I indicated above, the Epicureans and the Stoics offered similar understandings of the nature of happiness, that is, the maintenance of tranquility. However, they presented nearly opposed understandings of what it takes to maintain this state of tranquility and of the nature of the universe within which we are so tasked. While my comparison of these perspectives will necessarily be a bit cursory, we should be able to get some sense of how each conceived of the right way to live.

The Way Things Are: The Human Place in the Universe

Epicureans and Stoics agreed that the characteristic that sets humans apart from other beings is reason. Unlike other beings who are simply driven along unknowingly on the currents that direct the universe (gods excepted, of course), humans have the capacity to question, explore, and know, to some degree, the workings of reality. Because they can come to some understanding of the way things are, humans can come to some understanding of their place in the universe and adopt attitudes toward their own existence. Humans are *not*, for the Epicureans or the Stoics, free of the forces that govern reality; they are bound by those forces, as are all beings. But, they have a degree of freedom with regard to how they understand those forces and how they understand themselves in relation to them.

This basic agreement notwithstanding, the Epicureans and Stoics formulated radically different physics, that is, understandings of the universe and how it functions. Both Epicurean and Stoic physics were broadly materialist—there are no forces outside those that govern the material universe, and no reality beyond this one—but their characterizations of the function of those material forces could not be more different. Pierre Hadot explains:

> For the Epicureans, although bodies consist of aggregates of atoms, they do not form a true unity, and the universe is merely a juxtaposition of elements which do not blend together. Each being is an individuality—atomized, as it were, and isolated with regard to the others. Everything is external to everything else, and everything happens by chance; within the infinite void, an infinity of worlds is formed. For the Stoics, on the contrary, everything is within everything else, bodies are organic wholes, and everything happens by rational necessity. Within infinite time, there is only one cosmos, which repeats itself endlessly.[5]

Let's take a few moments to hash out these two very different understandings of reality.

Epicurus's most basic formulation of the nature of reality is as follows: "The universe is bodies and space."[6] What he meant, in short, is that reality is composed of two things: physical bodies and empty space. Perceptual experience proves to us that material bodies exist; after all, we encounter material objects daily, and we ourselves possess physical bodies. Everything else about the universe, Epicurus believed, can be derived rationally from this fundamental experience. Thus, Epicurus continues:

> And if there were not that which we term void and place and intangible existence, bodies would have nowhere to exist and nothing through which to move, as they are seen to move. . . . Furthermore, among bodies some are compounds, and others those of which compounds are formed. And these latter are indivisible and unalterable . . . they are completely solid in nature, and can by no means be dissolved in any part. So it must needs be that the first-beginnings are indivisible corporeal existences.[7]

While we do not technically experience empty space, its existence is necessitated by our experience of physical bodies; they have to exist somewhere. As for bodies themselves, we frequently experience them breaking into smaller pieces, indicating they are composites of smaller bits of matter. And, it stands to reason that there exist some fundamental, if nonpalpable, bits of matter that are themselves indivisible but are the building blocks of other, bigger material composites.

It has been suggested that Epicurus's physics is prescient of modern atomic science, but beyond superficial similarities, one needs to squint pretty hard to see anything like a contemporary scientific account of the universe in the Epicurean scheme.[8] Picture the Epicurean understanding of the universe this way: Imagine an infinite, open space occupied by an infinite number of elemental, indivisible bits of matter called atoms. Atoms are in constant motion within the infinity of the void. When atoms come in contact with each other they can either bounce off or glom onto each other. When they glom on, they form a composite with specific characteristics depending on the number and type of atoms that make up the composite. Lucretius explains the process thusly:

> . . . things come into being and, having come, can grow.
> Thus, clearly, the number of atoms of any type
> is infinite; and hence all needs are met. . . .
> And the more a thing possesses many traits
> and powers, the more it shows itself possessed
> of many kinds of atoms and different shapes.[9]

There are several salient features of this picture that we ought to highlight.

First, the fundamental existents of the universe, space and atoms, are infinite and eternal. Not only does space extend out infinitely in all directions, but it does not come into or out of existence; space has always been. The number (and possibly the type) of atoms is equally infinite, dispersed across the infinite expanse of "the void." Elemental matter, like infinite space, does not come into or go out of existence, *though the composites that are formed from elemental atoms are subject to dissolution and decay.* This last factor will become important in discussions to follow.

Second, the Epicurean universe is governed entirely by chance. Everything that is is the result of chance encounters of randomly traveling bits of matter as they collide with each other and bounce off, congeal into new types of matter, or break apart into smaller bits. All beings other than atoms and the void are the product of these chance encounters. And, because these chance encounters take place between infinite, eternally existing atoms in the medium of infinite, eternal space, the process of creation and decay is also infinite and eternal; *infinitely novel material realities are created eternally through the random encounters of elemental matter, that are then subject to eventual dissolution and eventual novel creation.*

Third, and most important for our discussion, the human being exists by virtue of this infinite, eternal process of chance encounter. Human beings are simply particular types of compounds composed of atoms whose characteristics are determined by those particular types of atoms. There is no overarching process governing the emergence of human life, no overarching providence overseeing the course of individual or collective human existence. While Epicurus believed in the existence of gods, he argued that they could in no way intervene in the course of events and would be disinterested in doing so even if they could. (The gods serve a purpose in Epicurus's account of the universe, but not as beings who take any interest in the course of human affairs; indeed, he argued it would be impious to think so.) Like all composite things, humans undergo the eventual dissolution of their material existence through a process we call death; death is the end of existence so that the matter composing the human being can be recycled into something new. In sum, *human existence is governed entirely by chance, and death is the absolute dissolution of that existence.*

If this account of the universe seems chaotic, frightening, and just a little crazy to you, you are not alone. The Stoic philosophers thought such a universe unlivable, and they proposed a nearly opposite account. In one of his letters, Seneca explains things in their most basic terms:

> As you know, we Stoics hold that there are two factors in nature which give rise to all things, cause and matter. Matter lies inert, susceptible to any use but yielding to none if no one sets it in motion. Cause, which is to say reason, shapes matter and turns it where it will, to produce various objects. For any object raw material and a maker are requisite; one is matter, the other cause.[10]

In this account, the universe is the material product of a cause, the deity, often identified with Zeus or Jupiter, who fashions base matter into everything that exists. Because the deity is rational, he creates with a plan, not haphazardly, and oversees all that happens through providence. Everything that happens happens for a reason, and, because the deity is omniscient, good, and completely rational, everything happens for the best. Marcus Aurelius puts it thus: "For there is one universe made up of all things, and one God who pervades all things, and one substance, and one law, one common reason in all intelligent animals, and one truth. . . ."[11] In short, *the universe proceeds exactly as it should according to the plan of the beneficent deity.*

Additionally, everything in the universe is interlinked with everything else. The system of causes works together to move the universe where it should go, and every existent in that universe functions together with every other within the whole. While beings other than the deity can serve as proximate causes in the creation of things and events, and human beings preeminently in this regard, their actions are part of a system of causation that regresses back to the ultimate first cause, the deity; they do not act spontaneously, but as part of a chain of causation initiated by the deity and according to the rational law of cause and effect that pervades the universe as such. *Every being has its place within the whole and contributes to the whole whether it knows it or not, including and especially the human being.*

Finally, the Stoics believed that base matter is eternal, as is the cause of the universe, the deity; however, the universe and all its components are in the process of constant change and ultimate decay. Thus, everything is in the process of passing out of existence, and, the Stoics thought, eventually this universe would cease to exist and be replaced by another. However, because there is one and only one eternal law governing the unfolding of all things, *the universe that eventually replaces the one we now occupy will look exactly like this one.* Marcus Aurelius counsels himself to meditate on the process:

> Constantly consider how all things such as they now are, in time past also were; and consider that they will be the same again. And place before thy eyes entire dramas and stages of the same form, whatever thou hast learned from thy experience or from older history; for example, the whole court of Hadrian, and the whole court of Antoninus, and the whole

court of Philip, Alexander, Croesus; for all those were such dramas as we see now, only with different actors.[12]

The universe that replaces this one will be populated by events that proceed exactly like the ones that have composed this universe. The figures drawn up into those events will look and behave exactly like the ones who were part of the events that compose this universe; for example, a court that looks exactly like the court of Hadrian will be governed by a figure who looks and acts exactly like our Hadrian and will be administered by others who look and act exactly like those who administered our court of Hadrian. Indeed, our court of Hadrian is simply a reduplication of past courts of Hadrian.

Comparing the two, the Epicureans offer us an infinite multiplicity of universes, each composed through the configuration of atoms as they randomly collide and form new substances; the Stoics offer us one single universe composed of matter and cause that continually replays itself for eternity according the rational law that infuses that universe, put there by the deity that governs that universe. The Epicureans present us with a universe of pure chance where we are utterly at the mercy of fortune and misfortune, where we must learn to navigate our way. The Stoic universe is one devoid of chance; everything happens by fate, by necessity of the law written into the universe itself. For the Stoic, fortune and misfortune are misrepresentations of reality that we project, misinterpretations that arise due to our refusal to occupy our preordained place in the whole. The question, then, is how to learn to live well in these alternate universes.

Happiness and How to Get It

As we can see, both the Epicurean and the Stoic philosophers presented a systematic and reasonably comprehensive account of the origin and nature of the cosmos reached through a sustained and intensive process of questioning and observation. Different as they may be, both traditions sought to explain the way things are and to place the human being in the universe in a meaningful way. As I have indicated throughout, however, the end of the philosophical endeavor is to allow the questioner to find happiness, to orient attention toward learning how to attune one's life to the way things are. Hadot explains:

> In Stoicism, as in Epicureanism, philosophizing was a continuous act, permanent and identical with life itself, which had to be renewed at each instant. For both schools, this act could be defined as an orientation of the attention.
>
> In Stoicism, attention was oriented toward the purity of one's intentions. In other words, its objective was the conformity of our individual will with reason, or the will of universal nature. In Epicureanism, by contrast, attention was oriented toward pleasure, which is, in the last analysis, the pleasure of existing.[13]

In opening up this understanding of philosophy as a way of living, as it is presented in the Epicurean and Stoic schools, I will address what happiness is, how to orient attention toward achieving it, and the types of *spiritual practice* developed by each school to assist the process of orientation.

As Hadot indicates above, for the Epicureans, happiness resided in an orientation toward pleasure. This doctrine earned the Epicureans a reputation for being gluttonous partiers, but this is clearly a misrepresentation of the Epicurean goal and surely the result of negative propaganda leveled at them by their competitors. Epicurus argued that humans, like all animals, are motivated by pleasure and the avoidance of pain; this idea, he thought, was obvious and not in need of defending. However, for humans, happiness is not secured by any and every pleasure. As Austin points out, "The desire for pleasure and aversion to pain come as standard operating equipment for animals. Epicurus, though, thinks the greatest pleasure is tranquility, a stable psychological state characterized by the presence of pleasure and the absence of pain."[14] And, because humans are rational animals, they have an increased capacity to determine and to seek those *stable pleasures* that are likely to last and bring a state of psychological tranquility, as opposed to *mobile pleasures* that come and go (and that leave dissatisfaction and discomfort in their wake). One of Epicurus's principal doctrines explains the difference between kinds of desire: "Among desires some are natural and necessary, some natural but not necessary, and others neither natural nor necessary, but due to idle imagination."[15] The good life involves securing the first kind of pleasures—and these can be boiled down to a surprising few: satisfaction of bodily needs, good friends, and contemplation of the universe—avoiding the last kind, and limiting the second kind.

Thus, the Epicurean art of living well involves cultivating a disposition Austin calls "hedonistic prudence," a habit of discerning and seeking those stable, lasting pleasures that lead to tranquility.[16] For example, treating oneself to a rich and expensive meal may present the lure of immediate and powerful pleasure, but a more prudential calculation reveals that one may suffer indigestion the next day and sticker shock when the credit card bill arrives. A more discerning take on pleasure might reveal that a simple meal shared with good friends yields more pleasure all things considered: satisfaction of bodily need, ease of digestion, low output of financial resources, and, more importantly, good conversation and strengthened bonds of friendship.

This art of living well does not come easy, however. Thus, the Epicureans developed a set of practices, or spiritual exercises, designed to help cultivate the correct attitudes and attention to the proper things. These practices included, first and foremost, memorization of and meditation upon the central tenets of the philosophy. To this end, Epicurus distilled his ideas into short collections of compact and easily memorized aphorisms. Later followers distilled these ideas even further into the famous Epicurean "fourfold remedy":

The Gods are not to be feared,

Death is not to be dreaded;

What is good is easy to acquire

What is bad is easy to bear.[17]

The Epicurean novice is also encouraged to recognize and reflect upon the nature of reality, and particularly his own impermanence in that reality. Such reflection was designed to relieve him of the fear of his eventual death since, from the Epicurean perspective, death is the dissolution of our existence and "that which is dissolved is without sensation; and that which lacks sensation is nothing to us."[18] Additionally, and as a result of the previous, the good Epicurean strives to live in the present and enjoy those things that life has to offer now. Finally, the Epicurean strives to cultivate a sense of gratitude for pleasures of existence, a strategy that is particularly effective for dealing with times of adversity. As Austin points out, "Taken together, we have three Epicurean points about misfortune: some losses are genuine misfortunes that merit grief, we should cope with our grief rather than seek to eliminate it, and the most effective strategies involve cultivating gratitude and caring friendships."[19] The point here is that good and bad fortune are a function of the chance nature of the universe: they have no rhyme or reason, and the individual deserves neither one nor the other. In troubled times one should remember better times with gratitude, bear misfortune with the support of close friends, and look forward with hope to better times to come.

For the Stoics, on the other hand, there is no such thing as misfortune; because the universe is governed by the rational law that is written into it by its creator, everything happens exactly as it should. The Stoic recipe for happiness, again, conceived as the preservation of tranquility, is to recognize this fact and to accept it. As Epictetus explains,

> Of all existing things some are in our power, and others are not in our power. In our power are thought, impulse, will to get and will to avoid, and in a word everything which is our own doing. Things not in our power include the body, property, reputation, office, and in a word, everything which is not our own doing. . . . Make it your study then to confront every harsh impression with the words, 'You are but an impression, and not at all what you seem to be'. Then test it by those rules you

possess; and first by this—the chief test of all—'Is it concerned with what is in our power or with what is not in our power?' And if it is concerned with what is not in our power, be ready to answer that it is nothing to you.[20]

Boiled down to its most basic formulation, this cardinal rule of Stoic philosophy states that our sole concern should be our attitudes toward and reactions to events; the events themselves are the effect of ineluctable fate. The Stoic's goal is to learn to control one's judgments about events, and the perfection of the Stoic life is to learn how to live within the bounds of what fate has determined.

As you might guess, this can be a tall order, and the Stoics developed a herculean set of spiritual exercises to accomplish this end of living in conformity with nature. These spiritual exercises primarily revolved around constant meditation on the nature of things. Indeed, the ideas of the most famous of the Stoic philosophers, Marcus Aurelius, come to us completely in the form of personal meditations, internal discourses that he compiled to aid in the task of learning to live well. While Marcus Aurelius's meditations are wide ranging, it is possible to locate a set of core strategies he employs. These include the following: (1) Focus on the fact that all things are in a constant state of metamorphosis; change and decay are the order of the universe. Thus, loss and death are natural processes that should not cause distress or mourning but should be accepted in stride. (2) Do not embellish experience with personal judgments but describe things in the most naturalistic, physical way possible. Marcus famously described sumptuous meals as the flesh of dead animals and royal robes as sheep's hair "dyed with the blood of a shell-fish."[21] Attending to things as they are ensures that we do not attach more value to them then they deserve. (3) Adopt the most comprehensive view of the situation possible, as if you are "viewing things from above." Taking this perspective reminds the meditator of the ultimate insignificance of human existence, of the "small part of the boundless and unfathomable time" allotted to each of us. (4) Finally, remember that you have been placed in this situation by fate, and the duties assigned by that place ought to be undertaken with purity of intention and in the interest of virtue.

For Epicureans and Stoics alike, the aim of happiness— *eudaimonia*, well-being, flourishing—rests in seeing one's life in the broader perspective of the way things are and learning to live accordingly. Philosophical practices are exercises designed to help us toward that end by offering an overarching account of the nature of reality and our place in it, turning our attention to the difference between those things over which we have control and those things over which we have no control, and orienting our efforts toward improving the things over which we have control—namely, our attitudes toward, judgments about, and responses to events. As different as these two philosophies are with regard to the nature of universe and the human place in it, the end of the good life is the same: maintaining tranquility by focusing on those things that depend on us and letting go of those things that do not depend on us.

POSTLUDE: WHAT DOES AND DOES NOT DEPEND ON US?

There is certainly something appealing about both the Epicurean and the Stoic accounts of living well. Their advice that happiness and well-being depend on attuning our lives to the way things are— attending to and improving those things we can control and changing our attitudes and judgments about those things we cannot—just seems right on some level. We ought to stop and question whether either offers an adequate account of the scope of things that do and do not depend on us, however. While it is surely the case that the appearance of evil is often an effect of our maladjusted judgments and subjective responses to events around us, there is something objective in our sense that genuine moral evils exist. While it is surely the case that unhappiness and the absence of flourishing are frequently the result of poor personal choices, there are cases in which some individuals suffer inordinately from injustices that are utterly independent of their choices. While it is surely the case that the maintenance of tranquility is a central ingredient in the recipe for individual well-being, it might be argued that tranquility in the face of systemic injustice is stolen flourishing, a privilege of the few that comes at the expense of the others. It is not clear that the Epicureans or the Stoics (or any of their ancient Greek and Roman philosophical competitors) provided adequate responses to these concerns; there are many reasons for this, and chief among them has to do with their rather narrow understanding of the scope of individual concern.

Hellenistic society accepted, and to some extent depended upon, a number of social arrangements that we ought to view as objectively unjust and intolerable. For instance, slavery was widely practiced in the Greco-Roman world. Slaves held no social status so long as they remained in the condition of indentured servitude, and, with very rare exceptions, women were deprived of public participation in society by virtue of their sex. Chronicling the situation of women in Roman society, Simone de Beauvoir explains that a woman is,

> . . . excluded from public affairs and prohibited from any "masculine office"; she is a perpetual minor in civil life. She is not directly deprived of her paternal inheritance but, through circuitous means, is kept from using it; she is put under the authority of a guardian. . . . Woman's first guardian is her father; in his absence, paternal male relatives fulfill that function. When the woman marries, she passes "into the hands" of her husband. . . .[22]

Neither the Greeks nor the Romans would have questioned the legitimacy of this reduced social standing of slaves and women. It would be very uncommon for women or slaves to gain admission to philosophical communities or to participate in philosophical discussions. (The Epicureans were outliers in this regard.) If one happened to be born into a position of reduced social standing, or to happen into one by circumstance, that limited his ability to seek and secure a good life, this fact would have been viewed as a matter of fate (or chance), and not as an injustice that should be remedied.

Because the Greeks and the Romans did not view these facts as systemic injustices, the only advice the Epicureans and the Stoics can offer for dealing with the fallout from these situations is to accept them as part of the way things are and, thus, to learn to live with them. More to the point, if the lack of avenues for social participation and self-determination cause you unhappiness, that is because you have not yet achieved the ability to attune your life to the way things are. But, surely, from a contemporary perspective, this sounds like blaming the victim; from our perspective, human beings deserve full recognition of their humanity and possess rights to access to social goods that make for happiness. Lack of full recognition and rights is an arbitrary arrangement that can and should be altered, not a matter of fate to be accepted. In short, *we have a broader understanding of the scope of human responsibility that encompasses not only our own well-being but that of others as well.*

Given this increased sense of the scope of human concern, defining living well in terms of the maintenance of tranquility seems narrowly self-involved, irresponsible, and complicit in systemic injustice. Living well requires more than seeing to our own *eudaimonia.* Attuning our lives to the way things are entails some commitments to the rights and well-being of others as well.

NOTES

1 Aristotle, "Nicomachian Ethics," bk. I, ch. 7, 1098a-15, in *The Basic Works of Aristotle*, ed. Richard McKeon, trans. W. D. Ross (New York: Random House, 1941), 943.

2 Aristotle did allow that there are some things that happen by chance, thus it is not meaningless to speak of fortunate and unfortunate events. He spoke of chance as a secondary kind of causation, as an *incidental cause*: "Things *do*, in a way, occur by chance, for they occur incidentally and chance is an *incidental cause*. But strictly it is not the *cause*—without qualification—of anything; for instance, a housebuilder is the cause of a house; incidentally, a flute-player may be so" (Aristotle, "Physics," bk. II, ch. 5, 197a 10, in McKeon,

ed., *The Basic Works of Aristotle*). In other words, the necessary cause of a house is the housebuilder; the housebuilder may, *by chance*, be able to play the flute. Hence, the flute player is an incidental cause of the house.

3   Emily A. Austin, *Living for Pleasure: An Epicurean Guide to Life* (New York: Oxford University Press, 2023), 9–10.

4   William B. Irvine, *A Guide to the Good Life: The Ancient Art of Stoic Joy* (New York: Oxford University Press, 2009), 33.

5   Pierre Hadot, *What is Ancient Philosophy?* trans. Michael Chase (Cambridge, MA: Harvard University Press, 2002), 129.

6   Epicurus, "Letter to Heroditus," in *The Stoic and Epicurean Philosophers: The Complete Extant Writings of Epicurus, Epictetus, Lucretius, Marcus Aurelius*, ed. Whitney J. Oates, trans. E. Bailey (New York: Random House, 1940), 4.

7   Epicurus, "Letter to Heroditus," 4.

8   Emily A. Austin, for instance, suggests, "The most striking feature of Epicurus' natural science is how much he got right. While the Stoics were trying to predict the future by reading the entrails of sacrificial birds, Epicurus was developing a remarkably modern account of the natural world" (Austin, *Living for Pleasure*, 203). It is difficult to know how far she would press the connection. While Epicurus's account seems closer to a modern scientific theory than divination from the entrails of animals, I would suggest that any deep similarity is largely illusory.

9   Lucretius, *On the Nature of Things*, bk. 2, 566–568, 586–588, trans. Frank O. Copley (New York: W. W. Norton, 1977), 42.

10 Seneca, "Letter 65," in *The Stoic Philosophy of Seneca: Essays and Letters*, trans. Moses Hadas (New York: W. W. Norton, 1968), 196.

11 Marcus Aurelius, "Meditations," VII, 9, in *The Stoic and Epicurean Philosophers: The Complete Extant Writings of Epicurus, Epictetus, Lucretius, Marcus Aurelius*, ed. Whitney J. Oates, trans. G. Long (New York: Random House, 1940), 536.

12 Marcus Aurelius, "Meditations," X, 27, 567.

13 Hadot, *Philosophy as a Way of Life*, 268.

14 Austin, *Living for Pleasure*, 28.

15 Epicurus, "Principal Doctines," XXIX, in Oates, ed., *The Stoic and Epicurean Philosophers*, 37.

16 Austin, *Living for Pleasure*, 34–39.

17 Hadot, *What is Ancient Philosophy?*, 123.

18 Epicurus, "Principal Doctrines," II, 35

19 Austin, *Living for Pleasure*, 159.

20 Epictetus, "The Manual of Epictetus, I" in *The Stoic and Epicurean Philosophers*, ed. Whitney J. Oates, trans. P. E. Matheson, 468.

21 Marcus Aurelius, "Meditations," VI, 13, 527.

22 Simone de Beauvoir, *The Second Sex*, trans. Constance Borde and Sheila Malovany-Chevallier (New York: Vintage Books, 2011), 99.

PART TWO

Thinking Philosophically

CHAPTER FIVE

Being, Teaching, Thinking

We have characterized the philosophical life as *asking the right questions with the goal of understanding the way things are to be able to attune one's life accordingly.* In line with the fundamental orientation of the book, this definition places primacy on the notion of *being philosophical* over the notion of *thinking philosophically.* While it is important to explore what it means to think in a philosophical manner, it is equally important to couch that manner of thinking in the concern for living in a particular way. In other words, our goal is to approach philosophy not primarily as a specialized form of investigation, as *a discipline,* but as the attempt to learn how to live well, as *spiritual discipline in the service of the good life.* Learning to *think* philosophically is part of this discipline.

So understood, aligning oneself with a philosophy represents a sort of apprenticeship. The would-be philosopher gives herself over to the fundamental teachings of the philosophical school. Becoming an Epicurean, for instance, entails more that adopting the view that happiness is secured through seeking pleasure and avoiding pain; rather, the Epicurean adept has learned how pleasure and pain fit into the scope of reality, has developed the ability to discern the difference between mobile and stable pleasures, and has mastered the practices that lead to tranquility of mind and body, the highest form of pleasure. Each of the schools developed its own pedagogical

forms. In many cases, those pedagogical practices were highly structured. One of the more pointed examples in this regard is the Stoic
educational scheme; the apprentice in Stoic philosophy underwent a
rigorous education in ethics, physics, and logic. In the Stoic account,
these three divisions of thinking are interlinked: learning to live
well (the goal of ethical education) entails learning to live in accord
with the structure of reality (the subject matter of physics) by coming to recognize that structure as rationally ordered (the purpose of
education in logic). While these three *disciplines* had to be taught
separately, the goal was to understand how they fit together into a
guide for living. In all cases, to advance in the philosophical life the
initiate submits to the pedagogical efforts of those more advanced
than herself. In so doing, she learns to think *philosophically* according to the guidelines of her chosen school.

So, learning to *think philosophically* involves, first and foremost,
adopting a certain perspective on the nature of reality and how to
live in it. While it is less likely, in our contemporary situation, that
a self-identified philosopher will align himself whole-heartedly with
a particular, established philosophical school, it is nonetheless likely
that he will have spent time engaging the perspectives of the established schools, allowing them to help shape his own perspective. If
he is genuinely philosophical, however, he will continue to examine
and question his adopted perspective and be willing to change it if
reasons present themselves.

Additionally, and in related fashion, good philosophers try to
hone their skills at communicating their ideas. A philosophy is only
as good as its ability to withstand dialogue with and criticism from
other philosophical perspectives. And, to the extent they remain
focused on the philosophical endeavor, philosophers are concerned
to better not only their own lives but also the lives of those around
them. (Philosophers sometimes stray from this mission into the more
self-serving activity of proving they are smarter than everybody else,
but at this point they stop being philosophers and begin to engage
in a different kind of discourse; more on this later.) Thus, learning
to think philosophically entails learning how to communicate ideas

effectively. In the contemporary setting, this art of communicating typically takes place, as in the present case, in writing. In the ancient and Hellenistic context, the place of the emergence of Western philosophy, the communication of ideas more frequently took place in oral form. In the Hellenistic period and up into the modern period, part of a philosophical education would involve learning how to advance and defend ideas in public dialogue—oral questioning and defense of philosophical positions—along the lines that Plato portrays Socrates in his dialogues. Such public dialogue represented a kind of "thinking-aloud." While we have become more dependent on writing as a mode of communication, much philosophical education still takes place in the form of discussion of philosophical ideas in philosophy classrooms. Part of becoming adept at "thinking-aloud" involves learning how to think methodically, and this ability entails breaking philosophical questions and topics into different types or divisions. This demand has led to the division of philosophy into distinct branches of investigation: epistemology, metaphysics, and ethics.

Etymologically, the term *epistemology*, translates roughly into "science of knowledge." Thus, to engage in epistemological investigations is to raise questions about *the nature and scope of human knowledge*. Such investigation is not the sole province of philosophy—cognitive scientists, among others, pursue these questions, too; but philosophers ask particular kinds of questions about our ability to know. For instance, is there such a thing as objective knowledge, that is, direct correspondence between reality and our ideas and beliefs about reality, or is knowledge always dependent upon and shaped by subjective factors like individual bias or cultural background? Is knowledge experiential—gained through the senses—or does it rest on the rational coherence of ideas? How much can we know and how much is beyond our limited mental capacities? Learning to ask the right kinds of questions is, thus, a matter of epistemological investigation.

Metaphysics raises questions about the nature of reality. The natural sciences also concern themselves with the nature of reality, but metaphysics addresses deeper issues than the origin and evolution of species or the processes of chemical reactions. Metaphysics deals with deeper structures of reality that account for the *way things happen and why they happen as they do*. The natural sciences operate out of an implied, but seldom acknowledged, metaphysic: mechanistic materialism, sometimes called "naturalism." In this sense, a metaphysic is a kind of underlying assumption about reality that grounds our explanations of the way things are. As we saw in our discussion of the Epicureans and the Stoics, differing metaphysical assumptions can yield radically differing accounts of the character of the universe and how to understand ourselves in it. Thus, to raise the question of how things really are beneath the surface of appearances is to engage in metaphysical speculation.

Ethics raises the question of what it means *to live well*. There are many different approaches to the question of how we ought to live. Those that we dealt with in the first part of the book were "eudiamonistic" accounts that argue that the good life is tied to securing individual well-being, but there are other contenders, among them "utilitarianism"—the notion that we ought, in all our actions, aim to produce the greatest amount of good overall, usually measured according to number of individuals positively affected by those actions—and "deontological" theories, which argue that proper action, and hence proper living, is action guided by moral duty. We will have opportunities to look at these differing accounts of the good life in chapter 8. No matter how living well is conceived, however, the exploration of how we ought to live and act is the province of ethics.

To engage with questions of how to think philosophically involves treating each of these branches of philosophical exploration. However, the central contention of this book, that *thinking philosophically* is couched within the broader problematic of *being philosophical*, makes exploring epistemology, metaphysics, and ethics in the abstract difficult and counterproductive. Thus, we will ground this treatment of thinking philosophically in a comparison of two actual living philosophical accounts, those of Platonism and Buddhism.

SOCRATES AND SIDDHATTHA

One of the major philosophical schools of the ancient Greek and Hellenistic period was Platonism. Platonism would eventually become a dominant force in the formation of Western civilization, due in part to the influence it exerted on the development of Christianity. Once Christianity became the ideological center of the Roman Empire over the course of the fourth century CE, and once Platonic philosophical ideas came to undergird Christian dogmatic formulations, the survival of some form of Platonism in Western thought was assured. Happily, much of the Platonic philosophical corpus has survived the ravages of history, and Platonism remains a principal philosophical position in contemporary philosophy.

Buddhism exercised a similar dominance on the development of civilization in East and Southeast Asia. While Buddhism's influence in India, the place of its original flowering, declined between the tenth and twelfth centuries CE, it became the principal cultural influence in the Lower Himalayan region, China, Japan, and the Indochinese Peninsula up to and beyond the modern period. Buddhism has travelled well in the contemporary world and is recognized as one of the major world religions. In Western intellectual contexts, Buddhism is more often treated as a religion than as a philosophy, but it takes little scratching beneath the surface to recognize that it is *no less philosophical* than the ancient and Hellenistic philosophies we have dealt with extensively to this point; if we conceive of a philosophy as a reasonably comprehensive account of the universe and the human place in it, then Buddhism stands up to just about any philosophical position out there. Nor is Buddhism *any more religious* than those same ancient and Hellenistic philosophies; most schools of Buddhist thought deny one of the defining characteristics of most religions, the existence of deities that control human affairs, while all the ancient and Hellenistic schools, in some way or other, require their existence. Thus, there is no good reason not to view Buddhism as a viable philosophical option to Platonism.

At the center of Platonism is the figure of Socrates, who serves as the protagonist of most of the dialogues written by his most famous pupil, Plato, the eponymous source of the Platonic perspective. An accurate picture of the historical Socrates eludes us for a number of reasons. First, Socrates left behind no written record of his life or thought; indeed, by most accounts, he was deeply suspicious of writing, thinking it brought communication to a standstill and undermined the capacity of memory. Thus, all the accounts we have of his life are second- and thirdhand, and these accounts are not altogether consistent. What is clear is that he had many admirers, many of whom counted themselves as his pupils, though those pupils took Socrates's teachings in many different directions, founding many different schools of thought espousing differing philosophical principles. Socrates also had many detractors and many enemies, and from them we get very different accounts of his character and his teachings. The composite sketch we can draw of his life is as such: Socrates was born into humble circumstances sometime around 470 BCE, in Athens; he lived his entire life there and rarely left the vicinity of the city except in brief stints as a soldier. He lacked consistent gainful employment and spent most of his time wandering the streets of Athens, typically barefoot and donning a worn cloak, engaging whoever would listen in conversation. He was remarkably ugly, though drew the affection and admiration of many despite this fact. Socrates eventually fell afoul of the authorities, was sentenced to death, and was executed in 399 BCE. The primary source we have for determining Socrates's philosophical ideas is in the writings of his disciple Plato. While Plato won the day in determining the contours of Socratic thought, Pierre Hadot suggests that we would likely have a very different picture of Socrates-the-philosopher had the works of the schools founded by other of his proteges survived.[1] For this reason, we designate the Socratic position "Platonism" rather than "Socratism."

A similarly elusive figure stands at the center of Buddhism, Siddhattha Gotama (sometimes spelled Siddhartha Gautama), who lived sometime during the sixth or fifth century BCE. The dates for his life are conventionally given as 566–486 BCE, but there is much scholarly debate about the accuracy of these dates. The biography of Siddhattha is equally inconsistent in the Buddhist account; there is no way to know whether this biography is reliable because, like Socrates, he left no writings; thus, again, the accounts of his life and teachings are second- and thirdhand. Siddhattha, the sources tell us, was born into privilege as a Nepalese prince; his father attempted to shelter him from the vicissitudes of life, but to no avail. Siddhattha was prone to wander from his life of luxury and, in these wanderings, encountered the disease, aging, and death that inevitably afflict human existence. With the goal of discovering the means of release from suffering, Siddhattha left the security of his palace life and took up education with various sages and ascetics, but without success. Philosopher Amber Carpenter narrates the end of this fruitless search, "On the verge of starvation, Siddhartha accepts an offering of food, sits beneath a pipal tree to meditate and wrestles with his demons—on some accounts for forty-nine nights—and in the morning he *understands*."[2] Such was Siddhattha's path to *enlightenment* or *awakening*, an understanding of the world that he initially thought was beyond his ability to teach to others. However, eventually he takes up the yoke of teaching a truth that promises release from the suffering of disease, aging, and death. Hereafter, Siddhattha would be known as the Buddha, or "enlightened one"; his teachings would be compiled and commented on for centuries to come, and eventually Buddhism—the Buddha's philosophy—would develop, much as Socrates's philosophy, into multiple schools of thought, some seemingly diametrically opposed.

Determining what constitutes the actual teaching of the Buddha is a difficult proposition. What Buddhists accept as the canonical teachings of the Buddha are secondhand collections (and in many cases more distant writings) of the Buddha's teachings, compiled centuries after his death, in what are called *sutras*. So, like Socrates, what we know of the Buddha's teachings are preserved, often in dialogue form, in the writings of his followers. But this is only the beginning of our difficulties.

Another complexity, at least from a Western philosophical mind-set, is that the standard method of attribution for determining what fits into the canon of the Buddha's teaching, that is to say, what is *buddhavacana* or the authentic word of the Buddha, is a good deal looser than in a Western context. Philosopher Jan Westerhoff explains:

> In the context of the history of Indian Buddhism during the first millennium CE, 'the teaching of the Buddha' is not just taken to comprise the discourses of early Buddhism [compiled in the first century BCE], but also a variety of other texts, such as the Mahayana *sutras*, as well as the *tantras* [first to eighth centuries CE]. All of these are traditionally considered to have been authored by the Buddha in some form or other, whether in his physical form during the present world-age (*kalpa*) as Buddha Sakyamuni during the time of his life in ancient India, or in another manifestation, or in another space and time altogether. . . . The Mahayana Buddhist tradition does not see the later origin of these texts as detracting from their claim to authenticity. It argues that these teachings were indeed authored by the Buddha, though not all were made public at the very beginning, as some doctrines would only be beneficial for beings that lived a considerable time after the Buddha's death. As such, the teachings were hidden until a suitable time for their propagation arose.[3]

The issue of attribution becomes more complicated still when one considers that the canonical teachings, known as the Pali Canon, comprise not just the actual discourses attributed to the Buddha (*suttas*), but also the monastic code governing the lives of Buddhist adepts (*vinyana*) and the philosophical elaboration of the Buddha's discourses in the *Abhidhamma* (the "higher teaching"), together comprising the *tripitaka*, or "three baskets" of the Buddha's teaching. The last of these—particularly important from a philosophical point of view—is particularly confusing from a Western point of view since it is viewed as *buddhavacana*, the authentic word of the Buddha, but not authored by the Buddha. Rather, the *Abhidhamma*, represents the word of the Buddha "mediated by disciples and other scholars," as scholar of Buddhism Maria Heim puts it.[4] The *Abhidhamma*, is a sort of elaboration of the what the Buddha meant even though he did not say it in those particular words.

All these complexities regarding the authentic *buddhavacana* might move one to look for the "real" Buddhist teachings, or the historical deposit of actual teachings propagated by the historical person, Siddhattha Gotama: a search for the historical Buddha, as it were. This urge to look to beginnings and to place greater weight on sources closer to the start of things is a Western assumption about the development of traditions of thought, one that views later developments as additions that obscure the initial clarity of the "true message." This is not a position that has been adopted by Buddhist practitioners, and Westerhoff suggests that adopting it is somewhat counterproductive for the historian of Buddhist philosophy: "The different emphases of the different traditions were shaped by the intellectual needs and circumstances of the times in which these traditions developed, and given the importance the Buddha accorded to teachings being suitable for the time, place, and audience that receives them, arguing against the authenticity of later teachings because they go beyond the discussions found in the early *sutras* is hardly satisfactory."[5] In a sense, the criterion of authenticity is placed more on whether the teachings express the Buddha's salvific message than on whether they faithfully convey what he literally said.

So, if we adopt convention, we are relieved of the task of determining what the historical Buddha really said. However, we avoid the Scylla of attribution only to fall in the Charybdis of scale: while the "Socratic canon" is relatively concise—comprising mainly the Platonic corpus—and temporally located in the fourth century BCE, the Buddhist canon is vast in size and composed over the course of many centuries. In addition to the canonical texts, we must recognize an even more vast compendium of philosophical commentary composed over the course of millennia that is critical to the development of Buddhist philosophy. This commentary was produced by Buddhist thinkers from different schools of Buddhist thought advancing different, often conflicting opinions on important matters of the Buddha's teaching. The scale of the Buddhist philosophical tradition makes it extremely difficult, if not impossible, to give a comprehensive account of the tradition, and we will not even try. Rather we will focus on the early, Theravadan tradition advanced in the *suttas* and *Abhidhamma* literature, not because it is more reliable than others, but out of convenience and due to its more limited scope.

I must stress that this comparison of Platonism and Buddhism is not intended in any way to be a comprehensive treatment of either. Rather, the two philosophies are meant to provide some perspective on the philosophical divisions of epistemology, metaphysics, and ethics. The best I can hope for is that our exploration will spur interest in you, my reader, to explore more on your own.

Our exploration of epistemology, metaphysics, and ethics will, therefore, be grounded in a conversation between Socrates and Siddhattha as their ideas are relayed to us in the writings of Plato and the early Buddhist tradition. There are good reasons for taking this direction. The similarly elusive nature of the respective founding figures is interesting in and of itself, as is the fact that what we have of their teachings comes to us through the interpretations of their followers. But more importantly, as Carpenter points out, both figures had a similar goal in their philosophical endeavors: "Siddhartha Gautama, Sage of the Śakyas, belongs with Socrates . . . in being motivated to reflection by pressing practical concerns. The compulsion to philosophy comes from the question 'How should I live?', and this is a question in which everything is at stake."[6] For both thinkers, any adequate answer to the question of how we should live requires *learning how to ask the right questions* so as to *understand the true nature of reality.* Their conclusions are very different, but the end of their respective philosophies is the same: *to learn how to attune one's life to the way things are.*

NOTES

1 Pierre Hadot, *What is Ancient Philosophy?* trans. Michael Chase (Cambridge, MA: Harvard University Press, 2002), 23.

2 Amber D. Carpenter, *Indian Buddhist Philosophy: Metaphysics as Ethics* (New York: Routledge, 2014), 1–2.

3 Jan Westerhoff, *The Golden Age of Indian Buddhist Philosophy* (Oxford: Oxford University Press, 2018), 11.

4 Maria Heim, "The Dhammasangani and Vibhanga," in *The Routledge Handbook of Indian Buddhist Philosophy*, ed. William Edelglass, et al. (New York: Routledge, 2023), 143.

5 Westerhoff, *The Golden Age of Indian Buddhist Philosophy*, 12.

6 Carpenter, *Indian Buddhist Philosophy*, 3.

CHAPTER SIX

Epistemology

What Is Knowledge? How Do We Know?

How Much Can We Know?

Humans tend to think they know more than they really do. In some cases, this confidence is a product of individual arrogance, but in many cases, it is simply a function of not stopping to consider what it means to know something. We generally understand that knowledge involves holding some form of cognitive attitudes about reality (also known as "beliefs"), and that those attitudes ought to correspond somehow to the way things really are to count as knowledge. But, how do those cognitive states form in our minds? In what ways and to what degree do they correspond to the way things are? How can we know whether they correspond to reality at all? Are there ways to test correspondence, and is there a threshold at which lack of correspondence signals ignorance? What is the line between knowledge, however limited, and ignorance?

These and many other questions arise once we raise the issue of what knowledge is. The stream of questions about how we know, what we know, how we know we know, and whether we can know anything at all, frequently leads individuals to abandon hope of finding answers, or simply to stop asking the questions in the first place. The philosopher, however, drives straight into the fray. While she knows it is unlikely that she will find answers to all the questions, she banks on the belief that pursuing questions is a better option than ignoring them and that getting some answers is better than having no answers. The branch of philosophy that treats questions about knowledge is called *epistemology*. Philosophers have reached general agreement on a standard definition of knowledge: *justified true belief*. In short, to make legitimate claim to know something is to hold a belief about it, a belief that is a true representation of that thing, and to have legitimate and defensible reasons for holding that belief. It sounds simple, but things rapidly get complicated as soon as we start asking what it looks like to hold a justified true belief.

First and foremost, what is a belief and how does it form? We all have beliefs, and we all need them to get through our day. Beliefs are our cognitive judgments and mental attitudes about ourselves and our surroundings, and they help us negotiate our way around the world. Imagine how difficult it would be to get around day in and day out without our general background beliefs about our surroundings! I, for instance, walk to work every day and must cross two busy intersections on my way. One of my functioning background beliefs is that people generally are bad drivers, easily distracted, and typically unobservant of pedestrians; while traffic laws indicate that I have the right of way so long as I am in a crosswalk following traffic signals, I remain cautious about stepping off the curb and vigilant while crossing because of this functioning belief. This background belief along with countless other related ones (drivers frequently ignore traffic signals; cars are hard and cause damage when they run into things; the United States is among the most expensive countries in the world for catastrophic health care, and so on) shape my daily behavior, and I am convinced they have saved my life on several occasions.

Now, this cognitive judgment that people generally are bad drivers is one that I carry around in my head. I am no longer sure exactly how it got there; it may be a belief that lacks any correspondence with reality—like the one I used to have as a child about evil, animated ventriloquist dummies living in the back of my closet. (That *Twilight Zone* episode really messed me up!) However, I am going to bet on the notion that people generally are bad drivers is not just a belief, but that it is a true belief. What makes me think so? Because it is confirmed frequently in my experience: At least once a week a driver makes a right turn on a red light, ignoring the walk sign and me preparing to step off the curb to follow it. At least once a month, a driver runs a stop light while I am in the crosswalk in the middle of an intersection. In the last five years, two people have been struck by cars while crossing one of the intersections I must cross (leading the town where I live to reconfigure the traffic signals to little avail). For these reasons and others, I am fairly committed to the notion that my belief is a true belief, that is, one that corresponds to reality, and more than this, a justified true belief. At this point, however, we need to stop and address what it means for a belief to be justified.

Claiming that a belief is justified means, first and foremost, that the one holding the belief has sound and defensible reasons for doing so. The question is not only whether my belief is true, but whether I have some good evidence for the belief being true; from a philosophical perspective, one cannot know things by accident. For instance, my childhood belief that ventriloquist dummies lived in my closet may have been true, but the point—one that my parents successfully convinced me of—is that I had no good reason to think they did; my belief lacked confirmation and, thus, true or not, did not rise to the level of knowledge. I have claimed firmer footing for my belief that people generally are bad drivers, namely, my frequent experiences of people driving badly.

Appeals to experience are a particular kind of justifying claim that falls under an epistemological theory called *empiricism*. Empiricists seem to have a strong case. What, after all, could serve as a firmer foundation for the justification of beliefs than the testimony of our senses. Yet, many philosophers have called into question the trustworthiness of sense perception. Our perceptions of things are easily compromised by optical illusions. We often perceive the same object differently in different environmental conditions. And, a growing body of research in psychology and cognitive science indicates that our perceptions are radically influenced by our internal emotional states, unconscious cognitive habits and perceptual shortcuts that are the product of our evolutionary heritage, and our own conscious and unconscious biases. There are good reasons, for example, to question whether my perceptions of things on my walk to work most mornings are completely trustworthy: I am not a morning person, so my walking-to-work mood surely colors my perceptions of others' driving; as my spouse points out, I am often quickly irritated and slow to extend the benefit of the doubt to other drivers in most situations. Given these facts, if I am willing to think about them, there are many reasons that make crossing the street perilous, and lack of driving skill in the general populace may be a minor one.

For this reason, many philosophers have claimed that empiricism is a poor candidate for a sound epistemology and have offered instead an alternative that goes broadly by the name *rationalism*. Rationalists argue that we ought to be skeptical of our senses and aim instead for rational coherence in our beliefs. How this coherence is established and evaluated differs among different rationalist positions, but in all cases, the rationalist argues that we ought to adopt some kind of rational principle or method to evaluate the legitimacy of our beliefs. So long as we apply this principle or method consistently and properly, we are more likely to form beliefs that are both true and justified.

Thus, for empiricists and rationalists, the process of forming justified true beliefs is different. For the empiricist, the formation of justified true beliefs is a sort of ad hoc, continuous process; beliefs arise from our experiences of the world, and they become more or less justified to the degree that they are confirmed by further experiences. Empirical knowledge is often referred to as *a posteriori knowledge*: justified true beliefs *proceed from* experiences and the justificatory process *comes from* the accumulation of further experiential confirmation. The rationalist, on the other hand, asserts that there are certain indubitable rational principles that must hold, and that any belief is justified, and hence true, because it conforms to those indubitable rational principles. For instance, if I have two apples and add two more apples, I have four apples; I know this is true by virtue of the indubitable mathematical principle that $2 + 2 = 4$. No matter how many times I add two apples (or oranges, or llamas . . .) and two apples (or oranges, or llamas . . .) I will get four apples (or oranges, or llamas . . .). I know this is the case because this is just how addition works. Rationalist knowledge is, thus, often called *a priori knowledge*; the principle that assures justified true beliefs *precedes or comes before* the formation of any particular belief and the belief is judged as justified and true based on its conformity to the preexisting principle.

In all cases, what we are up to when we raise epistemological questions is discerning the degree to which our mental understanding of and cognitive judgments about reality fit the reality we are trying to understand and make judgments about. In other words, we are trying to discern what we know, how we know it, and whether we know what we think we know. This last question—whether we know what we think we know—is a tricky one, however, because there are problems with both the empiricist and the rationalist accounts of knowledge that raise the question of the scope and accuracy of our knowledge. We have already addressed the central problem with empiricist theories, that our perceptions of reality are colored by external environmental factors and personal internal states. But, rationalism faces equally perplexing problems that raise doubts about its reliability. It is not clear, for instance, that indubitable first principles exist that possess the content to justify many of our beliefs; while the principle that $2 + 2 = 4$ is surely true, this principle gives me little information about how much caution I ought to employ in crossing the street. Other more content-laden rational principles, such as, "all things of the same type possess a common essence that determines what they are," are usually assumed rather than verified; in other words, they must be presupposed for there to be any possibility of knowing anything, and this makes them somewhat more dubitable than they often claim to be.

Given these perplexities, philosophers generally, though not unanimously, have adopted a viewpoint on human knowledge called *fallibilism*. As the name implies, this viewpoint states that *all human knowledge is fallible*; in other words, justified true belief is a more-or-less proposition. We aim at probability in our beliefs rather than certainty. The question of the scope of fallibilism in our beliefs introduces thorny issues into epistemology, however. Those who deny fallibilism suggest that any belief that lacks certainty simply cannot qualify as knowledge, but no uncontested foundation for absolute certainty has yet introduced itself, so this is a tough pill to swallow for epistemologists. At the other end of the spectrum, the Pyrrhonian Skeptics that we met in chapter 2 suggested that no beliefs are ultimately justified, hence we do not actually know anything, and should just suspend our judgments about reality as much as possible. David Hume, whom we also met in chapter 2, offered a mitigated Pyrrhonian position: while we cannot help but form beliefs, we ought to adopt a fair degree of epistemic humility with regard to them. A perhaps more palatable formulation of fallibilism was offered by the nineteenth century philosopher Charles Sanders Peirce (1839–1914). Broadly speaking, Peirce argued that knowledge proceeded through a process of empirical and methodological investigation; the natural sciences represent the quintessential example of such empirical and methodological investigation. So long as investigation remains public and follows the rules, we are on a path to convergence whereby established beliefs will lead eventually to correspondence with reality. However, we cannot know at any point where we are on that path or how far out convergence lies. Our knowledge is still fallible but getting closer to the mark.[1]

All this talk about knowledge, how we get it, and how we know we have gotten it is pretty abstract when discussed apart from any particular philosophical position. Hopefully these ideas will take on more contour and content by grounding them in actual philosophical positions.

PLATO'S "DIVIDED LINE"

Before proceeding with Plato's epistemology, it is important to address some complicating factors in his account of knowledge. First, though Socrates is the protagonist of most of Plato's dialogues, it is important to remember that Socrates did not write down any of his own ideas. It is difficult to know, therefore, how faithful Plato was to Socrates's thinking on things; he does not indicate whether or where he substitutes his own thoughts for those of Socrates. Thus, I will refer to the ideas presented as Plato's, even though they were articulated by Socrates in the dialogues.

Second, Plato's epistemology is intimately connected to his metaphysics and his ethics, so trying to treat it in isolation from these other concerns is complicated and somewhat artificial. While we will focus on his account of knowledge here, a complete treatment will require consideration of the nature of reality and the good life covered in chapters 7 and 8. Indeed, we will bump hard against his metaphysics at the end of this analysis to make sense of how Plato distinguishes knowledge from mere belief.

Finally, it is difficult to nail down exactly how Plato conceives of knowledge. He rarely focuses directly on the question of what knowledge is and how we attain it. One of the dialogues that deals most explicitly with knowledge, *Theatetus*, ends without a final resolution of the question. And there is a great deal of philosophical debate over Plato's epistemology. My interpretation, therefore, will be open for debate, but my hope is to provide some insight into the nature of epistemology by addressing Plato's ideas.

Perhaps Plato's clearest and most complete treatment of the issue of knowledge takes place in book VI of *Republic* in the image of the "divided line." We will focus on this image shortly, but before we can make sense of the image, we need to lay some groundwork. Central to Plato's epistemic concerns is the distinction between knowledge and opinion. For our purposes, opinion is synonymous with belief since an opinion is simply the expression of a belief or set of beliefs. In the dialogue *Meno*, amid a conversation about the nature of virtue, Socrates suggests to his interlocutor, the namesake of the dialogue, that sound opinion may be an adequate guide to a virtuous life even where actual knowledge of what is virtue is lacking: "Therefore true opinion is as good a guide as knowledge for the purpose of acting rightly. That is what we left out just now in our discussion of the nature of virtue, when we said that knowledge is our only guide to right action." It turns out that Socrates is being somewhat ironic in this statement, and Meno catches him out on this fact:

SOCRATES: So right opinion is something no less useful than knowledge.

MENO: Except that the man with knowledge will always be successful, and the man with right opinion only sometimes.

SOCRATES: What? Will he not always be successful so long as he has the right opinion?

MENO: That must be so, I suppose. In that case, I wonder why knowledge should be so much more prized than right opinion, and indeed how there is any difference between them.

Here is precisely the rub: What is the difference between true beliefs about something and knowledge of it? Comparing right opinion to the statues of Daedalus, the mythical sculptor whose creations were so life-like that they got up and wandered off, Socrates concludes:

True opinions are fine so long as they stay in their place, but they will not stay long. They run away from a man's mind; so they are not worth much until you tether them by working out the reason. . . . Once they are tied down, they become knowledge, and are stable. That is why knowledge is something more valuable than right opinion. What distinguishes them is the tether.[2]

Knowledge is true belief tethered to something, but to what? We get another example of the difference between knowledge and true opinion in *Theatetus*, a dialogue devoted to the question, "What is knowledge?" but ending paradoxically without any final answer. Using the example of a jury trial, Socrates engages Theatetus in the following conversation.

SOCRATES: And when a jury is rightly convinced of the facts which can be known only by an eyewitness, then judging by hearsay and accepting a true belief, they are judging without knowledge, although, if they find the right verdict, the conviction is correct?

THEATETUS: Certainly.

SOCRATES: But if true belief and knowledge were the same thing, the best of jurymen could never have a correct belief without knowledge. It now appears that they must be different things.

THEATETUS: Yes, Socrates, I have heard someone make the distinction. . . . He said that true belief with the addition of an account was knowledge, while belief without an account was outside its range. Where no account could be given of a thing, it was not "knowable"—that was the word he used—where it could, it was knowable.[3]

After several stabs at determining what would constitute an account of something securing knowledge of it and finding all of them faulty, the dialogue comes to an anticlimactic end. We are still left without any understanding of how a true belief could rise to the level of knowledge.

Let's stay with the example of the jury trial and see if we can reach any conclusions. On this account, the jury reaches its verdict based on eyewitness testimony. While none of the jurors *know* their verdict is true, they *believe* it is, based on the testimony of the eyewitness. Their verdict is nonetheless sound so long as their beliefs about the testimony are sound, even though they have no knowledge of the events. On this reading, it appears that the eyewitness is in the know; having witnessed the events and having formed beliefs about those events based on what she saw, we might say that she knows the truth about the events. The testimony of the senses tethers the beliefs about the events. There is reason to be suspicious of the testimony of the senses, however. We have already addressed the ways in which our perceptions of reality can be fooled by environmental factors or compromised by our various internal states. A growing body of evidence suggests that our reconstruction of past events in memory is even more unreliable, a factor that is particularly pertinent to jury trials. Plato is deeply suspicious of the senses, and for reasons that run much more deeply than those just listed.

In book V of *Republic*, Socrates compares philosophers, those lovers of wisdom whose goal is the acquisition of knowledge and truth, to the everyday, run-of-the-mill lovers of spectacles. He states, "The lovers of sights and sounds, I said, delight in beautiful tones and colors and shapes and everything art fashions out of these, but their thought is incapable of apprehending and taking delight in the nature of the beautiful in itself."[4] The lovers of spectacles engage the world entirely through the senses; they relish beautiful things and seek them out at every opportunity. In doing so, however, they conceive of Beauty (capital "B") solely in terms of beautiful things, and, when asked what makes this or that thing beautiful, can only point to characteristics of the thing itself. This musical composition is beautiful because of the complexity of its form. That painting is beautiful because of the artist's use of line and color. If asked how a composition's complexity or a painting's arrangement of line and color make it beautiful, the only answer is that complexity is a beauty-conferring quality in music and effective use of line and color is a beauty-conferring quality in paintings, but this is just circular reasoning. If asked how we can ascribe the same quality of Beauty to things like music and paintings (and chairs, and dogs, and people), the lover of spectacles is at a loss to provide the common denominator, and this is because he has mistaken beautiful things for Beauty in itself, according to Plato. Beautiful things are beautiful not because they *are* Beauty, but because they all *participate in* the reality of Beauty, the essence that *is* Beauty. At this point, we are getting close to the tether that binds true beliefs to knowledge.

In book VI of *Republic*, Socrates engages his dialogue partner, Glaucon, in a conversation about reality and the various cognitive capacities or functions through which we engage it. He asks Glaucon to imagine these capacities distributed along a divided line delineating the objects they are responsible for engaging. He asks Glaucon first to imagine the line divided in two; on one side of the line resides the visible world, or more broadly the perceptible world, on the other the intelligible world, the world of purely intellectual objects. He then asks Glaucon to again divide each side in two and place within the divisions a cognitive operation—imagination (Greek: *eikasia*), belief (*pistis*), thought (*dianoia*), and intelligence (*noasis*)—and its associated object.[5] So understood the line looks something like Figure 6.1.

The faculty of imagination, uncontroversially, concerns itself with images, broadly understood as imaginary objects. Somewhat more controversial, beliefs are formed only around perceptual objects; we will want to return to this in a moment. Intelligible objects are pure objects of thought, products of the proper use of reason. Intelligence, finally, is the faculty of discernment of the Forms; what Plato means by the Forms is complicated and will take up much of the analysis in the chapters 7 and 8. We will touch on their importance here regarding the role they play in his account of knowledge. For the time being, we can call them *essences*: beautiful things are beautiful, for instance, because they possess or participate in the essence of Beauty.

In point of fact, things are a good deal more complicated than this because Socrates asks Glaucon to imagine the line divided unequally, as in Figure 6.2.

Visible		Intelligible	
Imagination (*Eikasia*)	Belief (*Pistis*)	Thought (*Dianoia*)	Intelligence (*Noasis*)
Images	Perceptual Objects	Intelligible Objects	Forms

Figure 6.1 The Divided Line (version 1).

Visible		Intelligible	
Imagination	Belief	Thought	Intel-ligence
Images/Imaginary Objects	Perceptual Objects	Intelligible Objects	Forms

Figure 6.2 The Divided Line (version 2).

This is because, on Plato's conception of things, the visible world is populated by more things than the intelligible world is. And the imaginary world is much "bigger" than the perceptual one. The same is the case on the other side of the line. Let me explain.

The world of imaginary objects—chairs, giraffes, former presidents, mermaids, Harry Potter, and so on—is immense in comparison to the perceptual world. While chairs, giraffes, and former presidents can be perceived in addition to being imagined, mermaids and Harry Potter are purely imaginary objects. The realm of imagination, therefore, contains both things that are purely imaginary *and* things that can be both imagined and perceived. Because chairs and giraffes can be perceived as well as imagined, they have a slightly firmer footing in reality than mermaids and Harry Potter. The perceptual world is the realm about which I form beliefs. For instance, I believe that chairs are good for sitting on, giraffes have long necks, and the former president of the United States has just been indicted for conspiring to overturn the last election. My beliefs can be sound or faulty, true or false, depending on how carefully I perceive things and how much I keep my own powers of imagination out of play in making my judgments. (I can form beliefs about purely imaginary objects—for instance, governmental conspiracies that lack any shred of evidence—but they do not have a lot of traction when it comes to truth, and imaginary beliefs can cloud my judgment about perception.)

By comparison, the intelligible world is much less densely populated than the visible. For example, all the circular objects in my field of vision are instances—imperfect ones, geometers tell us—of the idea of a circle. The blue objects around the room I sit in—the binding of the book over there, my coffee cup—are various shades of the idea of blueness. Finally, the number of Forms is small compared to the number of intelligible objects I can form on the basis of them. We will come back to this last point in a moment.

What does this image of the divided line tell us about how Plato conceives of knowledge? Let's return to the example of a jury trial: recall that the jurors make their judgment of the case based on hearsay; in this case, we might say that they do not form beliefs about the events themselves, but rather must *imagine* themselves into the events based on the testimony of the eyewitness. Their beliefs are not so much beliefs about the events—which for them are purely imaginary objects—as they are beliefs about the testimony based on their perception of the reliability of the eyewitness. The eyewitness, on the other hand, has formed beliefs about the events herself and conveys those beliefs through her testimony. Given the general unreliability of eyewitness testimony, in what way could her beliefs about the events rise to the level of knowledge? To what must they be tethered to enter the range of the *known*? Let's turn to the example of Beauty and how it comes to be known, according to Plato.

I am of the opinion that the paintings of Mark Rothko are beautiful; in other words, I believe they are beautiful. (This, I find when I present Rothko's works to students in my philosophy of art classes, is a controversial belief.) How could this belief rise to the level of knowledge (provided it even makes sense to ask this question . . .)? One possibility is that I could survey all the other things I find beautiful, apply my thought to determine if there is a common denominator, and argue that Rothko's paintings are beautiful because they possess that common denominator; let's call that thing Beauty. In other words, I could think of knowledge as proceeding *empirically* from perception, through sound thinking, to knowledge; in this sense, knowledge of Beauty is the a posteriori outcome of the experience of beautiful things. This, however, is categorically *not* how Plato conceives things.

Recall Socrates's criticism of the lovers of spectacles. Their problem is that they mistake beautiful things for Beauty in itself and, as such, have no conception of what Beauty actually is. Thus, their beliefs about beautiful things, true as they may be, cannot constitute knowledge. In a counterintuitive way, one must know Beauty before one can accurately see it. In fact, the process is the reverse of that presented above, according to Plato. One must first know the Forms before they can become intelligible in thought and, thus, tether beliefs. The Forms are what beliefs must be tethered to in order to rise to knowledge, and this means that we must have some understanding of the Forms before we can form adequate beliefs. Plato fits squarely in the *rationalist* camp: knowledge rests on some a priori understanding that must somehow be possessed. But, how does an understanding of Forms end up in our heads (or wherever it ends up)? At this point we bump up against Plato's metaphysics, to which we must turn, briefly to complete the picture.

One answer to the question of where the understanding of the Forms comes from is the notion that they are simply innate, that is, we all are born with an understanding of them and, hence, already have them. But if this is the case, then there is no question about knowledge, no disputes over the question whether Rothko's paintings in fact *are* beautiful, for example. However, Plato clearly thinks that most people do not understand anything, so the notion that they are innate seems out of the question. The second option is that the Forms can be taught, that with the right instruction from the right philosopher one can come to understand them. But, Plato is pretty dodgy on the issue of whether the understanding of the Forms can be taught. Socrates characterizes his own mission as a philosopher not as an instructor of knowledge—he claims to know nothing himself—but as a midwife in the process of birthing wisdom. In a counterintuitive move, Socrates suggests that understanding of the Forms cannot be taught, but it *can* be learned. In his discussion with Meno over the nature of virtue, Socrates puts it thus:

Thus the soul, since it is immortal and has been born many times, and has seen all things both here and in the other [intelligible] world, has learned everything that is. So we need not be surprised if it can recall all the knowledge of virtue or anything else which, as we see, it once possessed. All nature is akin, and the soul has learned everything, so that when a man has recalled a single piece of knowledge—*learned* it, in ordinary language—there is no reason why he should not find out all the rest, if he keeps a stout heart and does not grow weary of the search, for *seeking and learning are in fact nothing but recollection.*[6]

Gaining understanding of the Forms is just a process of recalling what we already know but have somehow forgotten.

There are a number of metaphysical principles that are presented here at the end of our journey. We will lay these out briefly and take them up in more detail in chapter 7.

1. *The immortality of the soul*: The human soul is immortal and originally existed in a disembodied state in the intelligible world. In this state, the soul had immediate understanding of the Forms and, hence, knowledge of the true nature of reality. In the process of falling into a material body, the soul lost this understanding, at least any clear understanding, of what it knew in the intelligible world. Death is not something to be feared, therefore, but should be understood as a release from the world of ignorance and illusion.

2. *The theory of recollection*: Wisdom and understanding are not so much learned as recalled. The philosopher's task is not to teach understanding, but to rekindle it by bringing the individual, whether herself or another, to recollect what is already known.

3. *The theory of the Forms*: The Forms or essences of things are not just abstract ideas in our heads, they are real things.

Indeed, they are the only really real things; everything else is just a reflection or instance of some Form or other. To really know something is to look behind the appearance of the thing to see how it participates in a more real reality, its Form or essence.

Such is Plato's philosophical understanding of how one comes to a justified true belief: *holding a true belief that has been tethered to an understanding of its Form.* While Plato's account seems strange, it has nonetheless been extremely influential in Western thought. We turn now to the equally strange account that has been equally influential in the civilizations of East and Southeast Asia and beyond, the ideas attributed to Siddhattha Gotama, also known as the Buddha.

THE BUDDHA'S "FOUR NOBLE TRUTHS"

We confront complicating factors similar to those we encountered with Platonism, once we try to sort out what counts as knowledge in the Buddhist tradition. First, recall that the Buddha, like Socrates, did not write down his teachings; the teachings attributed to him are part of a canon of literature that was compiled after his death. Recall, as well, the wide berth that is given for what constitutes *buddhavacana,* the authentic teaching of the Buddha. For these reasons, it is important to recognize that the philosophical positions taken must be attached to specific schools of thought, rather than to the Buddha or Buddhism as such. While the views expressed are attributed to the Buddha, it is important to see them as the views of a particular form of Buddhism; we will stay as close as possible to the early, Theravadan tradition.

Second, the Buddhist account of knowledge, no matter what school of thought we address, is deeply tied up with the ethical concerns that undergird the Buddha's teaching. All schools agree that the central message of the Buddha's teaching concerns how we should live. The Buddhist's goal is to live a happy life, or more accurately stated, a life free from suffering; more accurately still, the end of Buddhist philosophy is release from suffering. To *know* anything, from this perspective, is to understand *that* we suffer, *why* we suffer, and *how* to end suffering. For this reason, we will have to continually index Buddhist epistemology (and Buddhist metaphysics in the next chapter) to Buddhist ethics. This means that Buddhist philosophy is a way of life in the same way as other philosophies we have addressed; the purpose is to ask the right questions so one can understand the way things are so that one can organize one's life in consonance with the way things are.

Buddhists are nearly unanimous in the conviction that the central teaching of the Buddha is the doctrine of the *Four Noble Truths*. How the Buddha came to this doctrine is inseparable from his biography, so we do well to remind ourselves of how he came to achieve enlightenment about the nature of reality. According to the tradition, upon being confronted by the reality of human suffering in the world, Siddhattha Gotama sought knowledge of how to escape that suffering. When guidance from others failed to provide this knowledge, Siddhattha meditated on the nature and cause of suffering and, at the end of his meditating, achieved awakening. His insight into the nature of human suffering was distilled into the Four Noble Truths that Siddhattha first shared with his followers:

> Now this, monks, is the noble truth of suffering: birth is suffering, aging is suffering, illness is suffering, death is suffering; union with what is displeasing is suffering; separation from what is pleasing is suffering; in brief, the five aggregates subject to craving are suffering.
>
> Now this, monks, is the noble truth of the origin of suffering: it is this craving that leads to renewed existence, accompanied by delight and lust, seeking delight here and there; that is craving for sensual pleasure, craving for existence, craving for extermination.
>
> Now this, monks, is the noble truth of the cessation of suffering: it is the remainderless fading away and cessation

of that same craving; the giving up and relinquishing of it, freedom from it, nonattachment.

Now this, monks, is the noble truth leading to the cessation of suffering: it is this Noble Eightfold Path; that is right view, [right intention, right speech, right action, right livelihood, right effort, right mindfulness,] right concentration.[7]

In short, the four noble truths are: (1) life is suffering, due to the general impermanence of all things; (2) suffering is caused by our desire for, craving of, attachment to those impermanent things; (3) the cessation of desire, craving, attachment leads to the cessation of suffering; (4) the way to end desire, craving, and attachment is practice of the Noble Eightfold Path. We will need to return to some of the ideas expressed here in chapters 7 and 8, in particular, the five aggregates and the Noble Eightfold Path; these ideas are central to Buddhist metaphysics and ethics. But, let's pause and analyze this central Buddhist truth about the nature, cause, and cessation of suffering.

From the Buddhist perspective, at least from the early Theravadan perspective, literally everything about life is suffering. Life's suffering can take many different forms—physical suffering caused by disease and aging, emotional suffering over loss and fear of death, mental dissatisfaction in the face of undesirable events, and so on—but in all cases, these life experiences boil down to a general unhappiness. Indeed, even happy and pleasurable events ultimately bring suffering because they do not last, and a sense of loss and dissatisfaction follows in their wake. If we subject this first basic truth to epistemic analysis, to hold any view other than this one, that life is suffering, is to live in ignorance; to believe it is to hold a true belief. However, the goal is not just to believe; the goal is to know and understand that life is suffering. The question, then, is whether and how one can come to an understanding of the veracity of the Buddha's claim about the universality of suffering.

Philosopher John Holder suggests that early Buddhist epistemology is best characterized as a form of *empiricism*, that is a process of reasoning from experience:

Experience figures prominently in the Buddha's teaching in at least three ways: first he taught that experience is the proper way to justify claims to knowledge—this is the heart of modern empiricism; second the experience of suffering is the motivation for seeking a religious path in life; and third, he provided a highly sophisticated psychological account of experience as a way of explaining how suffering arises, and how one might gain control over the causes of suffering so as to bring about the cessation of suffering. . . . Whereas most religious traditions are based on metaphysically speculative doctrines—doctrines for which there is little empirical evidence (e.g., the existence of a soul or the reality of heaven)—the Buddha told his disciples that one should believe only those doctrines that can be personally verified in experience.[8]

In short, if you want to verify that life is suffering, just look around: it is difficult not to recognize that there is a great deal of suffering, frustration, and dissatisfaction in life. And, it does not take a great deal of reflection on this fact to come to some understanding that at least one potent cause of that suffering, frustration, and dissatisfaction is our tendency to become attached to impermanent objects that we mourn the loss of; in other words, the first and the second noble truths are facts that are open to experience so long as we are willing to pay attention.

Early Buddhist epistemology is, therefore, quite different from the Platonic, rationalist suspicion of sense experience. It is not the case that Buddhism does not develop a metaphysical account of reality; indeed, the early tradition has a quite extensive metaphysics, one that becomes even more extensive in later Buddhist traditions (a topic we will explore in chapter 7). The Buddha taught, however, that this metaphysical account (most of it anyway) can be derived from experience, that in fact, our ability to derive metaphysical principles from experience is what ultimately assures their legitimacy. It is important, therefore, to pause and address the early Buddhist tradition's explanation of how experience works.

From the Theravadan perspective, experience functions on two distinct levels: a sensory level and an extrasensory level. At the most basic level, sensory experience is a product of the meeting of the sense organ and the sensory object. One discourse attributed to the Buddha explains it like this:

> Dependent on the eye and forms [vis. visible objects], eye-consciousness arises. The meeting of the three is contact. With contact as condition there is feeling. What one feels, that one perceives. What one perceives, that one thinks about. What one thinks about, that one mentally proliferates [vis. forms cognitions of].[9]

In the case of visual experience, perception is a function of the contact between the eye and the visual object; that contact then results in the visual sensation, perception, and ideation about the visual object. The same is the case with the other senses: hearing, smell, taste, touch, along with a sixth sense in the Buddhist scheme, mind sense—collectively known as the "six sense bases." In a sense, experience is an outcome of the interactive process that takes place between an experiencer and an experienced thing; our consciousness of and beliefs about our experiences are a product of that interaction. We might visualize as in Figure 6.3.

What "contact" between the sense organ and the sensible object means is not completely clear; Buddhist philosopher Peter Harvey suggests that we understand contact in terms of stimulation. Thus, sense stimulation is the product of the interaction of the sense organ and the sense object. Stimulation then gives rise to sensation, perception, and cognition. (There is one critical aspect of this model that we

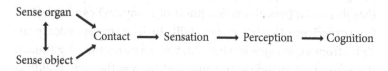

Sense organ

Sense object

Contact ⟶ Sensation ⟶ Perception ⟶ Cognition

Figure 6.3 Buddhist Account of Sensation and Cognition.

need to take note of regarding the position of the experiencer: there is no essential "I" that exists behind the experience, no Platonic soul, no subject that "has" the experience. From the Theravadan perspective, the person is, as Holder points out, "an integrated psycho-physical process."[10] In an important sense, we might characterize the experiencing subject as a product of the experiential event. We will need to return to this point in chapter 7.)

Alongside sensory experience is a deeper kind of extrasensory, introspective, or intuitive experience. This is the kind of experience that the Buddhist adept develops through the mastery of deep meditative states. The knowledge gained through this kind of introspective, meditative experience is of a more subtle kind than that reached though sensory experience. Holder characterizes these different levels of knowledge as the difference between "knowledge *how*" and "knowledge *that*": the development of sensory experience can show *how* suffering arises due to attachment to and craving of impermanent things and even, to some extent, *how* the cessation of attachment and craving means to the cessation of suffering; meditative experiences yield a deeper knowledge about why this is the case, knowledge *that* all things are impermanent, including myself, because they are part of a dependent, causally conditioned process of mutual interaction. This introspective knowledge is genuinely liberating knowledge, as Holder explains, "Liberating knowledge . . . is achieved by mastering the knowledge (*how*) that transforms the way the mind processes experience so that suffering does not arise and also by knowing *that* everything that exists is a dependently arisen (and so an impermanent) process. . . . Thus, these supersensory powers are not supernatural powers, but best thought of as extensions of ordinary human sensory powers that can be achieved by someone who has a mind that is developed by meditative practices."[11] Liberating knowledge is knowledge into the deeper structures of reality that reveals that impermanence runs all the way down; unlike the Platonic account, there is no enduring foundation upon which things are built, no essences, just the process of continually dependent arising.

We are delving pretty deeply into Buddhist metaphysics at this point; this notion of dependent or conditioned arising will occupy us in chapter 7. To summarize our treatment of epistemological concerns, early Buddhist epistemology is broadly empirical in nature: experience—both sensory and meditative—is the path to knowledge. Mastering our senses and disciplining the mind through meditation are the keys to achieving justified true beliefs. It is important to recognize a pragmatic aspect in Buddhist epistemology, however; genuine knowledge is always knowledge that leads to liberation from suffering, and hence knowledge of how we should live. The standard by which we judge the adequacy of ideas is, ultimately, whether they lead to the cessation of suffering by cultivating a mindful way of living. We will return to this standard in chapter 8.

POSTLUDE: ON THE DIFFERENCE BETWEEN PHILOSOPHIZING AND BULLSHITTING

Princeton Professor Emeritus of Philosophy Harry Frankfurt could not have known when he wrote his essay, *On Bullshit*, that his reputation would be made by his detailed and erudite treatment of this subject matter. While one wonders whether Frankfurt might have been engaging in some of what he analyzes in the essay, one of its effects has been to give philosophers an analytic distinction to differentiate what they are doing—searching for truth—from what they are frequently accused of doing—pushing hot air, pedaling snake oil, bullshitting.

Frankfurt defines bullshitting as a kind of deceptive speech act that falls somewhere on a spectrum between bluffing and lying. A classic example of bluffing is the practice of trying to pass off a losing hand as a winning one in poker, but this is too structured an activity to tell us much about what bluffing really involves. A better example of bluffing is the often reported frustration of graduate students at the way some of their colleagues tend to engage in class conversations: some graduate students frequently have the annoying habit of bluffing their way through classes, pretending to know more about a topic than they do, repackaging the ideas of others (typically the ideas of other graduate students) without acknowledging where the ideas come from, in order to garner the positive attention of their professors. If I engage in this kind of bluffing there is clearly some deception going on, but it does not really involve the content of my speech. Rather, I am being deceptive about myself; I am trying to pass myself off as something I am not. Lying is a different sort of deception because the liar's deception concerns precisely the content of what he says. He says something other than what he believes to be true with the intention of convincing someone that he believes it is true. In this sense, the liar's speech is related to truth in a way that the bluffer's is not.

Frankfurt most clearly identifies what constitutes bullshitting by contrasting it with lying. The liar requires some orientation toward truth while the bullshitter could not care less about the difference between truth and nontruth. Frankfurt explains:

> It is impossible for someone to lie unless he thinks he knows the truth. Producing bullshit requires no such conviction. A person who lies is thereby responding to the truth, and he is to that extent respectful of it. When an honest man speaks, he says only what he believes to be true; and for the liar, it is correspondingly indispensable that he considers his statements to be false. For the bullshitter, however, all bets are off: he is neither on the side of the true nor on the side of the false. His eye is not on the facts at all, as the eyes of the honest man and of the liar are, except insofar as they may be pertinent to his interest in getting away with what he says. He does not care whether the things he says describe reality correctly. He just picks them out, or makes them up, to suit his purpose.[12]

In this sense, the bullshitter is closer to the bluffer than the liar; the bluffer is not really oriented to the truth either. But, bullshitting seems somehow more pernicious than bluffing. The bluffer attempts merely to pass himself off as something he is not; bullshitting seems to disfigure reality itself if it succeeds. Recent politics in the United States may be a case in point.

Socrates was often accused of engaging in something like bullshit because his questioning seemed to lead in all directions except the topic at hand. In one of Plato's dialogues, Callicles, in the middle of a discussion of how to live well, bursts out, "Shoes! You keep talking nonsense. . . . By heaven, you literally never stop talking about cobblers and fullers and cooks and doctors, as if we were discussing them."[13] But we need to stop and ask whether Socrates's obfuscations really count as bullshit, at least as Frankfurt presents it. One easy way to do so is to compare the Socratic/Platonic project with that of a group of competitors in the ancient and Hellenistic periods, the Sophists. Hadot explains that the Sophists were a group of professional teachers who, for a price, taught how to master language for public use; "For a salary, they taught their students the formulas which would enable them to persuade their audience, and to defend the *pro* and the *contra* sides of an argument with equal skill. . . . They taught not only the technique of persuasive discourse, but also everything which could help the individual attain that loftiness of vision which always seduces an audience. . . ."[14] In short, the Sophists were consummate bullshit artists, and they charged a price to pass on the art of bullshitting to others. In comparison, Socrates's evasiveness looks very different.

Surely, Socrates dissembles in the dialogues, adopting the opposite strategy of contemporary graduate students, ironically claiming to know less than he does, playing the dolt in need of education from those more informed than he. Socrates bluffs in a way, but in the service of something other than getting away with it. Socrates remains oriented toward the truth, even in the midst of his dissembling, and this signals the difference between philosophy and bullshit: the philosopher cares about the truth above all else.

The Buddha was certainly no bullshitter, and based on the teachings attributed to him, he was not very ironic either. But we get some sense of his commitment to the truth in one of his discourses where he likens his teachings to a raft. Just as a raft is useful for crossing from one river shore to the other, so the Buddha's teachings are useful for passing from the shore of ignorance to the opposite shore of knowledge. But what ought one do with the raft once he has crossed the river?

> When that man got across and had arrived at the far shore, he might think thus: "This raft has been very helpful to me, since supported by it and making an effort with my hands and feet, I got safely across to the far shore. Suppose I were to haul it onto the dry land or set it adrift in the water, and then go wherever I want." Now, bukkhus, it is by doing so that that man would be doing what should be done with the raft. So I have shown you how the Dhamma [vis. teaching] is similar to a raft, being for the purpose of crossing over, not for the purpose of grasping.[15]

Once you find the truth, you no longer need the teaching. You also get better at recognizing bullshit. . . .

NOTES

1   For a concise treatment of Peirce's ideas, see Robert Burch, "Charles Sanders Peirce," last modified February 11, 2021, *Stanford Encyclopedia of Philosophy*, Sanford University, https://plato.stanford.edu/entries/peirce/.

2   Plato, "Meno," 97b-e, in *Plato: Collected Dialogues*, ed. Edith Hamilton and Huntington Carins, W.K.C. Guthrie, (Princeton, NJ: Princeton University Press, 1961), 381–382.

3   Plato, "Theatetus," 201b-d, in *Plato: Collected Dialogues*, ed. Edith Hamilton and Huntington Cairns, tr. F. M. Cornford (Princeton, NJ: Princeton University Press, 1961), 908.

4   Plato, "Republic," 476b, in *Plato: Collected Dialogues*, ed. Edith Hamilton and Huntington Cairns, tr. Paul Shorey (Princeton, NJ: Princeton University Press, 1961), 715.

5   Plato, "Republic," 509e-511e, 745–747.

6   Plato, "Meno," 81c-d, 364 (*emphasis added*).

7   "The First Discourse," in *In the Buddha's Words: An Anthology of Discourses from the Pali Canon*, ed. Bhikkhu Bodhi, trans. Bhikkhu Bodhi and Nayanaponika Thera (Boston: Wisdom Press, 2005), 76.

8   John J. Holder, "A Survey of Early Buddhist Epistemology," in *A Companion to Buddhist Philosophy*, ed. Steven M. Emmanuel (Malden, MA: Wiley Blackwell, 2016), 224–225.

9   *"Madhupindika Sutta*, The Honeyball," in *The Middle Length Discourses of the Buddha*, ed. and trans. Bhikkhu Bodhi (Boston, MA: Wisdom Publications, 1995), 203.

10 Holder, "A Survey of Early Buddhist Epistemology," 232.

11 Holder, "A Survey of Early Buddhist Epistemology," 236.

12 Harry G. Frankfurt, *On Bullshit* (Princeton, MA: Princeton University Press, 2005), 56–57.

13 Plato, "Gorgias," 490e, in *Plato: Collected Dialogues*, ed. Edith Hamilton and Huntington Cairns, trans. W. D. Woodhead (Princeton, NJ: Princeton University Press, 1961), 273.

14 Pierre Hadot, *What is Ancient Philosophy?*, trans. Michael Chase (Cambridge, MA: Harvard University Press, 2002), 13.

15 *"Alagaddupama Sutta*: The Simile of the Snake" in *The Middle Length Discourse of the Buddha*, ed. and trans. Bhikkhu Bodhi (Boston: Wisdom Publications, 1995), 228.

CHAPTER SEVEN

Metaphysics

What Is There? Why Is It There? How Does It Work?

A common questioning strategy in a game of twenty questions is to start with the question, "Animal, vegetable, or mineral?" This question helps classify the object under consideration and helps determine the next kinds of questions we should ask about it; for instance, if the answer to the question is "mineral," indicating that the object is inanimate, it would be imprudent to include among follow-up questions "Does it have fur?", since fur is generally associated with animate objects of the type "animal." Therefore, it would be highly unlikely, though not impossible, that a mineral-type object would have fur. This simple question—"Animal, vegetable, or mineral?"— banks on several assumptions that take us a long way toward figuring out the object at the heart of the game. One, very useful, but often overlooked, assumption is that there are *things* out there that are open for public observation and that are subject to collective agreements.

A second assumption is that things differ from each other such that it is possible to pull out one thing from the vast array of other things and attend to it; however, if we were confronted with a simple collection of things that are all different from each other, the game would grind to a halt; given that the set of things is extensive enough to make a game of twenty questions at all interesting, it would be difficult if not impossible to sort out what particular thing is in question in the batch of different things. Happily, focused attention reveals that things are not just different from each other, but some *kinds* of things share similarities; things tend to fall into recognizable groups or *categories* that help us organize what is otherwise just a collection of random stuff. For instance, to question whether something is animal, vegetable, or mineral first splits the totality of observable things in two according to whether the object is living or inanimate. It then divides living things into two categories according to whether the thing is a sentient being or non-sentient life form. This capacity to organize things into various groupings by attending to certain characteristics they share helps make understandable what would otherwise be a heap of different objects standing willy-nilly next to each other.

A third assumption is that the characteristics we use to determine different types of things are the relevant ones and that our *categories are reasonably comprehensive and generally shared*; this is an assumption that does not always pan out. Let me give an example: I recently discovered, when I spoke with her about this example of playing twenty questions as a way to make sense of the branch of philosophy called metaphysics, that my spouse had never played twenty questions. When I explained the "animal, vegetable, mineral" strategy, she asked, "What if the object is a straw hut? Does that count as vegetable or mineral?" (My spouse is also a philosopher, and one thing philosophers are good at is raising questions that throw wrinkles into the game.) Here's one wrinkle: it is not completely clear that our categories can be fine-grained enough to account for everything there is; of course categories can be tweaked or altered to better capture things. But, this raises an even stickier question: Are categories in any sense real or definitive, or are they just ad hoc constructions we adopt to carve things up?

Think of metaphysics as a refined game of twenty questions; when we engage in metaphysics, we attempt to explain the nature of things and types of things, how and why things are the way they are, and how things hang together to shape reality. Concerning the nature of things, for instance, we might raise the issue of *parts and wholes*;

most things we encounter are, in fact, composites of smaller things. This fact raises several questions regarding the nature of the thing: Is the composite the more real thing or the components that make up the composite? Is the composite real at all, or is the really real level of reality more elemental, indivisible bits of matter? Or the reverse, are the bits really nothing—just random stuff—until they have formed into something? Reality looks very different, philosophically speaking, depending on how one answers these questions.

Concerning the nature of types or categories, we might ask how it is that they come about. Are they fundamental realities that preexist the things we group them under? The notion that categories are real and preexist the things they categorize is a position known as *realism*. A realist, as the name suggests, argues that categories are essences or archetypes that determine the fundamental nature of things; if we ask which is really real, the categories or the things categorized, a realist sides with the categories, since the things categorized are only what they are because of where they fall in the archetypal scheme. *Nominalists* argue something close to the opposite position; categories do not preexist the things they categorize, rather categories are constructed, a posteriori, from the characteristics of things we deem relevant. As the designation suggests, categories are like names we give things. They are not realities and, hence, do not mark out essences; they are ad hoc devices that help us make sense of the pile of things out there. Again, depending on where one falls on the realist-nominalist spectrum, if we can think of it as a spectrum, one has a very different viewpoint on the nature of reality. A realist will argue that categories are universal realities that exist *ante res* ("before objects") whereas the nominalist will conceive categories as existing *in rebus* ("in objects"); however, it is possible to be a realist (arguing that categories are real) *and* argue that universals exist *in rebus*—Aristotle was a case in point.

If we turn our attention to the question of how and why things are the way they are, an equally intriguing set of questions comes to mind. Where, for instance, do things come from? Most philosophical positions that posit the existence of gods or other kinds of superhuman beings—aliens or interdimensional beings, for example—suggest that reality, that is, all the things there are, was brought into existence through the creative activity of these superhuman beings. There are several ways to conceive of this creation: Perhaps the god or gods made everything from preexisting stuff. Or, perhaps, the god or gods brought the stuff that things are composed of into existence and then, directly or indirectly, fashioned things out of it. Several philosophical positions that arose between the first century BCE and the second century CE, collectively designated "gnostic," argued that the material universe is the ill-begotten creation of an inferior god; this material reality is the source of evil in the universe, and the human goal is to recognize that we belong not to this material existence, but to another, more pure, spiritual realm. Of course, creation philosophies are only one option; other philosophical positions argue, for instance, that the reality we know is the product of random forces that collude to shape things as we know them. Things could just as well have been other than they are. The secret to happiness is recognizing this fact and learning to live with it.

The goal of all this questioning is to determine how things hang together. Depending on what answers are given to the questions, things hang together in a certain way, and reality has a particular shape. In other words, the goal of metaphysics is to figure out how things really are. As I have argued throughout this volume, this goal brings with it a further end: determining how to live in accord with reality. In this sense, metaphysics is geared to the good life. Let's address how these questions get worked out in Platonism and Buddhism.

PLATO'S "THEORY OF FORMS"

We bumped up against Plato's metaphysics at the end of the chapter 6. The central idea that grounds Plato's perspective is the theory of Forms. Exactly what Plato thought about the Forms and how extensively he worked out the theory is a matter for debate. Like most of

Plato's philosophical perspectives, he rarely addresses the theory of Forms directly, but in relation to other questions, and the account of the Forms and how they work shifts and develops over the course of the Platonic corpus; the picture of the Forms gets worked out in a dialogical manner, and Socrates is the protagonist in these dialogues. In short, a full-blown account of the theory of Forms is an educated guess based on a reconstruction from multiple dialogues.

We get some sense of the way Plato conceives of the Forms and how they function in his discussion of art in book X of *Republic*. In this section of the dialogue, Socrates asks Glaucon to consider how it is that a couch would come to be represented in a painting. Obviously, the painter represents a couch in his painting, but what is the status of that couch? Somewhat counterintuitively, Socrates suggests that the represented couch is "three removes" from the true couch. To sort out why this is the case, we need to consider different types of craftsmen-of-couches: In a way, the painter is a couch-craftsman; he creates a couch, but the one he creates is a representation, a copy or "imitation" (*mimesis*) says Socrates, of another couch, the one produced by the carpenter. If the carpenter's couch were the true couch, then the painter's couch would be only one remove from the true couch, but Socrates claims that it is three removes; how can this be? It turns out that the carpenter's couch is already one remove from the true couch, the couch produced by the master-couch-craftsman, God:

> Now God, whether because he so willed or because some compulsion was laid upon him not to make more than one couch in nature, so wrought and created one only, *the couch which really and in itself is.* But two or more such were never created by God and never will come into being. . . . [I]f he should make only two, there would again appear one of which *they both would possess the form or idea,* and that would be the couch that really is in and of itself, and not the other two. . . . God, then, I take it, knowing this and wishing to be the real author of the couch *that has real being and not some*

particular couch, nor yet a particular cabinetmaker, produced it in nature unique.[1]

The true couch, then, is the one made by God; the carpenter then takes as her model for a couch the one that God created. If the carpenter is a good one, the couches she makes are faithful reflections of the couch God made, but they are still one remove from the true couch, particular manifestations of the archetype that determines what a couch is. We can visualize things as in Figure 7.1.

Here, then, we have some sense of the role that Forms play in Plato's metaphysics: they are the genuine article, the ultimate level of truth. Particular couches made by particular carpenters are one remove from the true Form of the couch made by God; they are reflections of the Form. The couch made by the painter is an imitation of the carpenter's couch; but, why is it three removes from the true couch, and not just two? The painter's couch is not a faithful representation of the carpenter's couch and simply cannot be because the painter can only capture one perspective of the couch. Thus, his painted couch is an *appearance* (one remove) of an *imitation* (two removes) of a *reflection* (three removes) of the true couch. The painter can only capture appearances that have little to no relation to truth.

If we map this discussion of art onto Plato's image of the divided line that we explored in chapter 6, we get a clearer sense of what is going on. Recall that the divided line can be visualized as in Figure 7.2.

The painter is, by definition, a creator of *images*; his objects are objects of the *imagination* and, hence, have no relation to reality.

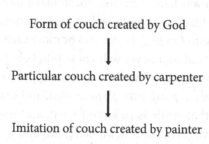

Figure 7.1 Plato's Theory of Forms.

Visible		Intelligible	
Imagination	Belief	Thought	Intelligence
Images	Perceptual Objects	Intelligible Objects	Forms

Figure 7.2 The Divided Line.

The carpenter, on the other hand, is a maker of particular *perceptible objects*. Her couches may be good or bad ones, but, in all cases, they are patterned on some idea of what a couch should be. We might be able to *think* about many different ways a particular couch might look; these might entail differences in particular dimensions, particular colors, particular materials, and so on, but a couch just has to have a distinct *form* in order to function as a couch. Thus, we have the idea (*form*) of what a couch really is, particular conceptions of possible (*intelligible*) couches, material (*perceptible*) couches, and *images* of couches. Taken together, the Form that defines what a couch is and ideas about possible couches are real; visible couches, whether material or imaginary, are at best reflections of real couches.

This notion that purely intelligible objects are more real than concrete, particular objects seems peculiar. Plato offers several arguments in defense of the position, however. For one thing, Forms are immutable (unchanging) and eternal (unaffected by time) while concrete objects are not. The particular couches in my house have been the objects of years of abuse by now-adult, male, children; they started off as pretty good couches, but I would no longer recommend them as ideal for use as couches. Also, because material objects are changeable, they are impermanent and eventually cease to be altogether; my couches are now well on the way toward this state of "no-longer-being." *The Form of couch is impervious to such damage and unaffected by the ravages of time, and this immutability and eternality makes it, for Plato, more real than the physical couches in my house.*

A second and related argument for the reality of Forms over concrete particulars is that Forms are "self-subsisting" entities, that is to say, they are what they are independently of anything else. Another way of putting it is that the Form of a couch simply is what a couch is; it defines those "couchy" properties that make couches couches. All other couches *are* couches because they have the property of "couchiness" displayed in or possessed by the Form; in other words, particular couches are not self-subsisting, but are what they are by virtue of their relation to the Form. It is certainly odd to speak of the property of "couchiness" that makes couches "couchy." The Form of Beauty offers a less odd example. Recall our encounter with the lovers of spectacles in chapter 6: they are unable to understand what beauty is because they mistake Beauty for beautiful objects. On Plato's understanding, beautiful objects are beautiful because they "partake of" or "participate in" Beauty (the Form). Plato/Socrates makes the case more directly in the dialogue, *Phaedo*, "If someone tells me that the reason why a given object is beautiful is that it has a gorgeous color or shape or any other such attribute, I disregard all these other explanations . . . and I cling simply and straightforwardly . . . to the explanation that the one thing that makes that object beautiful is the presence in it or association with it, in whatever way the relation comes about, of absolute beauty."[2] A Rothko painting, therefore, is beautiful not by virtue of any particular attribute it possesses, but because it is associated with, participates in, or partakes of the Form of Beauty, however that association, participation, or partaking happens. In short, *the Form of Beauty (or couch) exists "in-itself," and as such really is, while beautiful (or couchy) things exist by virtue of their relation to the Form.*

A corollary of this argument is that particulars can be more or less what they are depending on how closely they are associated with or participate in or partake of the Form that defines what they are. For instance, the couches in my house are still . . . barely . . . recognizable as couches, but in comparison with the nice new ones in the showroom of the local furniture store, they are significantly less "couchy." I am quite fond of my daughter's childhood paintings and find them beautiful, but they are not at all beautiful compared to a Rothko; for many art critics, a Rothko is positively ugly compared to Botticelli's "Venus." (I disagree with both of these critical assessments, by the way, but this discussion will have to wait.) *The Form of couch and the Form of Beauty, on the other hand, can never be anything other than the absolute exemplar of what they are, and this, for Plato, is another argument for their being more real.*

In summary, then, Plato offers a two-tiered account of reality that we can picture as in Figure 7.3. The intelligible is a kind of transcendent, immaterial realm filled with things that are unchanging and unaffected by temporality. As such, the intelligible realm provides a stable foothold in reality that stands out against the change and impermanence that we encounter in daily existence. That daily existence is lived out in the perceptible realm of material things. Unlike the intelligible, the perceptible realm is characterized by change and impermanence, and these characteristics make the perceptible realm less real than the intelligible realm from the Platonic perspective. Indeed, perceptible things only exist at all by virtue of their participation in or relation to intelligible realities.

If we read these ideas back into the general metaphysical questions we raised at the beginning of this chapter, it is safe to say that Plato is a metaphysical *realist* in the strongest possible sense. The categories we use to group material things—the Forms—are real, indeed, they are the really real things. The Forms exist *ante res* and they determine and ground the existence of particular material things. Concerning the question of *parts and wholes*, Plato seems to side with the idea that composite things are more real than the stuff they

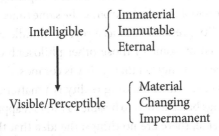

Figure 7.3 The Intelligible Realm and the Perceptible Realm.

are composed of given that material objects become less what they are as they decompose into their constituents—as my couches are quickly in the process of doing. If we ask where things come from, Plato is a little elusive in offering an answer. Because the Forms are eternal and immutable, they cannot come into or pass out of existence; in other words, they are there in the intelligible realm from the beginning. Because perceptible, material objects are what they are because of their relation to, or participation in, the Forms, we should assume that the Forms perform some causal function in bringing about material things, but Plato never gives a firm or direct explanation to what the causal relation is between Forms and material particulars, though later followers of Plato offer many different causal explanations.

One gets the sense, reading Plato's dialogues, that he never completely worked out the theory of Forms in its entirety. One reason for this is probably because Plato's bigger project is to offer some picture of how we should live; his metaphysical project is in the service of something more important: an ethical account of the good life. This account will be a focus of chapter 8.

THE BUDDHIST DISTINCTION BETWEEN "CONVENTIONAL" AND "ULTIMATE" REALITY

It would be difficult to imagine a more different metaphysical picture to the one offered by Plato than that offered by Buddhism. Buddhism developed in conversation with a number of competing philosophies that were all developing in India around the same time. The Buddhist account of reality presents itself as a sort of "middle way" between extremes offered by some of those other philosophical positions. At one extreme is the notion that reality is composed of substantial things; in this case, understanding reality is a matter of discerning how those things behave so as to be able to interact appropriately. At the other extreme, there are no things; the idea that things exist is the product of an illusion and the goal is to see through the illusion to find liberation from the bonds that hold one to the illusion that things really exist.

Philosopher Noa Ronkin argues that the Buddhist picture of reality is best conceived as a form of process metaphysics: "Underlying process metaphysics is the presupposition that encountered phenomena are best represented and understood in terms of occurrences—processes and events—rather than in terms of 'things,' and with reference to modes of change rather than to fixed stabilities. The guiding idea is that processes are basic and things are derivative. . . ."[3] In response to the claim that reality is composed of substantial things, early Buddhists thinkers, the Abhidharmikas, responded that what appear to be things are really processes. In response to the idea that there are no things, only the illusion of things, the Abhidharmikas responded that things are not merely illusory, even if they are better understood as processes than substantial realities.

Thus, Buddhism offers the notion that there are really two "truths," or two "realities," or two ways of conceiving of reality: *conventional reality* and *ultimate reality*. Conventional reality is the designation for our common, everyday engagements with the world. We occupy a world that seems to be occupied by things—couches, chariots, locust trees, llamas, human beings, and so on. We can see and feel these things and frequently bump into them, and they feel pretty substantial. Beneath the conventional, however is another, more fundamental, ultimate level of reality that is responsible for the existence of those conventional things and the ways they behave. Thus, Buddhism offers a sort of two-tiered, universe that initially looks something like the Form–matter one that Plato offered: the things that we see and interact with depend, for their existence, on another level of reality. However, ultimate reality in the Buddhist metaphysical scheme looks very, very different from the Platonic realm of Forms.

One important difference is the way the conventional is related to the ultimate. The relation is not characterized by association or participation, but rather in terms of composition: conventional things are composites while ultimate reality is populated by non-composite "absolute simples" called *dhammas* (also known as *dharmas*[4]). This relation between conventional and ultimate is explained in an important early Buddhist text called the *Milindapañha*. This text recounts a conversation between the Buddhist sage Nagasena and a king named Milinda. The conversation begins when King Milinda asks Nagasena "how he is known," in other words, who he is. Nagasena responds that he is known as Nagasena, though "Nagasena is only a name, since no person is apprehended here." In short, though he is named Nagasena, the name does not name any person. Milinda then asks how it is the case this particular person standing before him, with all these particular attributes—"the teeth, the skin, the flesh, the sinews, the bones, the marrow, the kidneys, the heart . . ."—who is named Nagasena is not Nagasena; it appears, Milinda suggests, that Nagasena is telling a fib. Rather than answer the king, Nagasena turns the tables and asks Milinda where is the chariot he used to travel to see Nagasena:

NAGASENA: Are the wheels . . . the body of the chariot, the flagstaff, the yoke, the reins or the goad the chariot?

MILINDA: O no, venerable sir.

NAGASENA: But then, sire, is the chariot the pole-axel-wheels-body-flagstaff-yoke-reins-and-goad?

MILINDA: O no, venerable sir.

NAGASENA: But then, sire, is there a chariot apart from the pole-axel-wheels-body-flagstaff-yoke-reins-and-goad?

MILINDA: O no, venerable sir.

NAGASENA: Though I, sire, am asking you repeatedly, I do not see the chariot. Chariot is only a sound, sire. For what here is the chariot? You, sire, are speaking an untruth, a lying word. There is no chariot. . . .

MILINDA: I, venerable Nagasena, am not telling a lie, for it is dependent on the pole, dependent on the axel [and all the other parts] . . . that the chariot exists as a denotation, appellation, designation as a current usage, a name.

NAGASENA: It is well; you, sire, understand a chariot. Even so it is for me, sire. . . .[5]

In short, we cannot say that the chariot (or Nagasena) is any one part of the chariot (or Nagasena), or all the parts taken together, or something other than the parts taken together, at least in any ultimate sense. Rather, the chariot (and Nagasena) is a collection of things assembled in a particular way and conventionally named "chariot" (and "Nagasena").

Philosopher Amber Carpenter derives a philosophical principle from this tale that she calls the CHARIOT PRINCIPLE: "Whatever has constituents depends upon those constituents for its existence, and depends upon conceiving this 'many' as a 'one' for its unity, and so does not exist ultimately, but only (at best) conventionally."[6] In short, calling something by a conventional name like "chariot" or "Nagasena" involves conceiving of some batch of things existing in roughly the same place and assembled in a particular way as a single thing; the conventional object is really an assemblage, a grouping of objects that we take as a single object for the sake of convention. And, because the things that compose the conventional object—things like wheels and flagstaffs for chariots and teeth and kidneys for persons—are themselves composites, they are just as conventional as chariots and persons. The CHARIOT PRINCIPLE runs all the way down: "The upshot is that nothing complex can be ultimately real; the only fundamental constituents of reality, out of which each part, and each part of a part, and so on, is constituted, are absolute simples."[7] What, then, are these ultimate simples, called *dhammas*, and how do they work?

Philosopher Jan Westerhoff describes *dhammas* as particularized properties that exist absolutely independently of anything else and manifest entirely locally. They can be physical—composed of the basic elements of earth, fire, water, and air—or non-physical—mental states like feelings, volitions, and cognitions. Westerhoff continues,

Particularized properties differ from properties as ordinarily conceived (sometimes called universals) in not being present at multiple locations at the same time. While the same universal red can be present at the same time in a postbox in London and a flag in Beijing, the particularized property of redness of this postbox is present only here, at this place and time, and the particularized property of this flag is present only there, at that place and time. The two particularized properties might be very similar, but they are not the same, and they are distinguished by their respective space-time locations.[8]

In this sense, the *dhammas* are fundamentally different than Platonic Forms. Recall that what makes beautiful things beautiful, for Plato, is that they all participate in the universal Form of Beauty. Similarly, what makes red things red, in a Platonic framework, is their participation in the Form of Redness. In the Abhidharmika metaphysical framework, Westerhoff notes, "Each *dharma* has its specific characteristics (*svalaksana*) that distinguish it from every other *dharma*, and it has these characteristics as an intrinsic nature (*svabhava*)."[9] Thus, different red things are particular instances of redness because part of what constitutes them are particular *dhammas* with red characteristics.

This account of ultimately reality can be extremely disorienting and difficult to conceive because any particular thing, conventionally understood, is really just an assemblage of particular *dhammas* that happen to have come together in this particular way, at this particular place, on this particular moment. We experience things as substantial objects because our sensory apparatus (which is itself a composite of *dhammas*) is not fine-grained enough to discern what is going on at a more fundamental level. (Understanding of this deeper sense of reality is the fruit of Buddhist practices of meditation and mindfulness that we will discuss in chapter 8.) The distinction between conventional reality and ultimate reality yields some other metaphysical principles that we need to briefly address here. We will address these in more detail in the next chapter.

1. *Conditioned arising* or *dependent origination*: Conventionally understood "things," that is, objects that are available to human experience, are not the independently existing things they appear to be but are really the effects of a

causally conditioned arising. In other words, everything that exists at the conventional level of reality originates and is dependent on the particular assemblage of *dhammas* that happen to compose it. Apart from the *dhammas*, there are no independently existing substances, but rather causal processes of assemblage.

2. *Momentariness*: *Dhammas* are not only localized in space such that every instance of red, for example, exists independently and separate from every other instance of the same shade of red. *Dhammas* are also "localized" in time. In other words, every instance of red is a momentary instance that flashes out of existence the moment after it arises. Westerhoff explains, "Each *dharma* lasts only for a moment, but gives rise to a new *dharma* very much like it in the moment immediately after it, much like one frame in a film is succeeded by a very similar one. Our powers of temporal discrimination being what they are, they cannot distinguish the successive similar *dharmas*, and experience them as a single, continuous phenomenon."[10] In sum, just as objects, conventionally considered, are not independently existing, substantial things existing in space but conditioned processes of assemblage, neither are they temporally continuous things, but sequences of momentarily arising processes.

3. *Impermanence*: All this means that Buddhist metaphysics conceives of reality as impermanent. We all experience the impermanence of things; things change and pass out of existence all the time. We experience and mourn the death of loved ones and the loss of cherished objects. But, in the Buddhist account, impermanence is much more radical. Things are constantly shifting in and out of existence beneath levels of experience that we are capable of. In this sense, large scale, macroscopic levels of change and impermanence are really an effect of microscopic processes of continual change and impermanence.

4. *No-self*: Again, apart from the *dhammas*, there are no independently existing things. It is difficult even to see the *dhammas* themselves as meaningfully existing independently given that they are momentary apparitions that pass out of existence as soon as they arise. Another way to put this point is that there are no *self-subsisting* beings in the Buddhist metaphysical scheme. This is the case from couches to chariots and from trees to human beings.

Thus, human beings, like everything else, lack unity and self-subsistence. The human self is a composite of five *khandhas* (or *skandhas*): form, feeling, perception, volition, and consciousness. The *khandhas* themselves are aggregations or "bundles" of *dhammas* and, as such, exist as sequentially occurring, momentary assemblages of conditioned arising. The person is not a distinct thing but, as John Holder puts it, "an integrated psycho-physical process."[11] The human being is an aggregation of aggregates of *dhammas* and, therefore, characterized by the same kind of impermanence as everything else in the universe.

Lack of self-subsistence is a particularly jagged pill to swallow because human beings want to conceive of themselves precisely as self-subsistent, independent *persons*. That is to say, humans experience themselves as independent *selves*, and like to consider themselves as such. However, the attachment to things, including and especially the idea that I am an independent self, is the source of suffering that Buddhism promises to remedy. Recall the Four Noble Truths we addressed in the last chapter: (1) life is suffering, due to the general impermanence of all things; (2) suffering is caused by our desire for, craving of, attachment to those impermanent things; (3) the cessation of desire, craving, attachment leads to the cessation of suffering; (4) the way to end desire, craving, and attachment is practice of the Noble Eightfold Path. Attending to things, including and especially oneself, as if they are self-subsisting entities, rather than impermanent and momentary processes of conditioned arising is the cause of suffering; cessation of this tendency leads to the cessation of suffering, and cessation of this tendency is what the Noble Eightfold Path aims at. The end is the recognition that there is no persistent, self-subsisting nature to things, including and especially this thing I call "me," "myself," "I."

If we place these Buddhist claims in the broader discussion of general metaphysical questions we get a sense of how different this perspective is from the Platonic one. Regarding the question of whether things are best characterizes as *wholes* or according to their *parts*, the clear answer is that parts are real; the *dhammas* are the ultimately real things, while the composite wholes are at best conventionally real. Likewise, the Abhidharmikas lean toward *nominalism* when it comes to categories or types: things like chariots and persons are just names we assign based on convention. Concerning the question of where things come from, they are but the sequence of momentary assemblages of *dhammas*. While Plato characterizes the most fundamental level of reality, the Forms, as a stable, unchanging, and eternal foundation, the Abhidharmikas characterize ultimate reality in terms of instability and constant change.

By comparison, the Buddhist picture is quite disorienting and, perhaps, distressing, but in some ways this is the point. The end of Buddhist understanding and practice is to come to an experience of no-self and to end suffering, suffering that extends, we will discover in chapter 8, across multiple lifetimes. We can think of suffering in two ways, one passive and the other active. In one sense, suffering is simply the nature of existence; because all things are subject to the processes of conditioned arising and impermanence, all things suffer the consequences of cause and effect and passing away. In this way, we can say that existence generally is affected by a kind of passive suffering. This is just the nature of things from the Buddhist perspective.

However, some portions of reality pile suffering upon suffering by adopting a kind of dysfunctional perspective on suffering. Sentient beings like humans, who tend to operate out of a sense of self, have a proclivity to mistake conventional reality for ultimate reality. In doing so, they become attached to things, including and especially themselves, and they lament when those things change, break, become old, and eventually pass out of existence. This is a sort of active suffering that sentient beings like humans take upon themselves. While the passive kind of suffering is an unavoidable factor of existence, the active kind of suffering is absolutely avoidable if one can cultivate the right kind of viewpoints and attitudes. Beyond a metaphysical perspective on reality, Buddhism is a set of practices that aims to instill those right kinds of viewpoint and attitude. We will explore this aspect of Buddhism in chapter 8.

POSTLUDE: IS CONVENTIONAL REALITY REALLY REAL?

The metaphysical pictures offered by Plato and the Abhidharmikas seem to devalue the conventional viewpoint of our everyday experience and dismiss it as having any fundamental foothold in genuine reality. If we take Plato's allegory of the cave seriously, experienced reality is merely shadows of a more genuine reality; to the extent that we place stock in everyday experiences, we are like prisoners chained in a cave of illusions. According to the Abhidharmikas, conventional experiences of composite things as unified, permanent objects is the source of suffering that can be ended only by recognizing the ultimate reality of no-self. To what extent, then, should we be at all concerned about conventional reality as anything other than something to be abandoned?

The dominant readings of Platonism and Theravadan Buddhism interpret the theory of Forms and the distinction between conventional and ultimate reality as *ontological* accounts, that is, accounts of *being* or the way things are. Thus, Plato's theory of Forms presents the Forms as existing in a separate, transcendent realm from the everyday realm of matter. These realms are opposed to each other according to the characteristics of their respective inhabitants; the Forms, being immutable and eternal, are real, while sensible objects, being changeable and affected by time, are at best imperfect reflections of formal realities. By the same token, in the Buddhist perspective, the *dhammas*, as absolute particulars that compose conventional objects, are ultimately real; composite things, that is, things that are available to our everyday experience—things like chariots or persons, are, as Westerhoff suggests, "merely mental fictions superimposed on conglomerations of fundamental objects. . . ."[12] In all cases, our conventional experiences of things are false impressions that keep us bound to something we should want to escape.

There are, however, alternative and compelling readings of these metaphysical texts that suggest that the theory of Forms and the distinction between conventional and ultimate reality are not ontological accounts of the way things are so much as *phenomenological* accounts of our experience of the way things are. In other words, the ultimate end of these accounts is to focus attention on the ways we experience reality and to transform that experience in such a way that we might live better. Concerning the Buddhist distinction between conventional and ultimate reality, Maria Heim argues:

> My own reading is to take seriously the possibility that the intellectual purpose of the canonical Abhidhamma is to offer a complex set of analytical practices and methods that allow the practitioner to explore the many—perhaps infinite—facets of experience without ever landing on a final, single, essential list of the contents or aspects of it. . . . This is philosophy of a different sort than metaphysical assertion and argument. It is a practice of exploring and transforming experience within the therapeutic and soteriological aims of Buddhist dogma.[13]

In a similar way, philosopher, Eric Perl, offers a kind of phenomenological reading of Plato's theory of Forms:

> What Plato presents . . . is not two worlds, a world of sensible instances on the one hand and a world of transcendent forms on the other, but rather one world, that of intelligible form, and the appearances of that world which constitute sensibles. . . . The transcendence of the forms . . . is not the separation of

one world, one set of objects, from another, but is rather the priority of and independence of intelligible reality in relation to the sensible appearance of that reality, and is thus a transcendence which does not contradict but rather both implies and is implied by immanence.[14]

These phenomenological interpretations surely need far more explanation than I can provide here. The point to these interpretations is to raise the possibility that Platonic and Buddhist metaphysics is not so much about trying to give a comprehensive account of reality as exploring the various ways in which we conceive that reality and, further, to show that some conceptions are more conducive to living well than others.

The distinction between ontological and phenomenological readings may seem, on some level, to be a distinction without a difference. If some conceptions of reality are better than others, then do ontology and phenomenology—the way things are and the way we experience the way things are—not boil down to the same thing in the end? There may be something to this criticism, but I think there is one important difference to be highlighted: ontological readings urge us to disregard the conventional reality we live in day-in-and-day-out. Ontological interpretations label the conventional as not really real, and hence not an object of concern. However, does living well not entail some responsibilities toward some of the beings with whom we share conventional reality, at the very least other sentient beings? We will return to this question.

NOTES

1   Plato, "Republic," 597c-d, in *Plato: Collected Dialogues*, ed. Edith Hamilton and Huntington Cairns, trans. Paul Shorey (Princeton, NJ: Princeton University Press, 1961), 822, *emphasis added*.
2   Plato, "Republic," 100c-e, 80–81.
3   Noa Ronkin, "Theravada Metaphysics and Ontology," in *Buddhist Philosophy: Essential Readings*, ed. William Edelglass and Jay L. Garfield (New York: Oxford University Press, 2009), 14–15.

4   In Indian Buddhism, ideas were developed in two different, but closely related languages, Pali and Sanskrit. The early canonical writings that we are focusing on were composed in Pali, and I have tried to stay close to the Pali designations of ideas. Some of the material I am quoting uses the Sanskrit designations. This will be the reason for slight shifts in terminology.

5   "Extract from the *Milindapañha*, 'Milinda's Questions'," in *Buddhist Philosophy: Essential Readings*, ed. William Edelglass and Jay L. Garfield (New York: Oxford University Press, 2009), 273. Dialogue speaker names added.

6   Amber D. Carpenter, *Indian Buddhist Philosophy: Metaphysics as Ethics* (New York: Routledge, 2014), 43.

7   Carpenter, *Indian Buddhist Philosophy*, 43.

8   Jan Westerhoff, "Metaphysical Issues in Indian Buddhist Thought," in *A Companion to Buddhist Philosophy*, ed. Steven Emmanuel (Malden, MA: Wiley Blackwell, 2013), 130.

9   Westerhoff, "Metaphysical Issues in Indian Buddhist Thought," 130.

10 Westerhoff, "Metaphysical Issues in Indian Buddhist Thought," 133.

11 John J. Holder, "A Survey of Early Buddhist Epistemology," in *A Companion to Buddhist Philosophy*, ed. Steven M. Emmanuel (Malden, MA: Wiley Blackwell, 2013) 232.

12 Westerhoff, "Metaphysical Issues in Indian Buddhist Thought," 132.

13 Maria Heim, "The *Dhammasangani* and *Vibhanga*: The Perfectly Awakened Buddha and the First Abhidhammikas," in *The Routledge Handbook of Indian Buddhist Philosophy*, ed. William Edelglass, et al. (New York: Routledge, 2023), 154.

14 Eric Perl, "The Presence of the Paradigm: Immanence and Transcendence in Plato's Theory of Forms," *The Review of Metaphysics*, 53, no. 2 (December, 1999): 352.

CHAPTER EIGHT

Ethics

Good and Bad, Right and Wrong, Moral and Immoral

I will go out on a limb and argue that everyone wants to live well. Nobody, so far as I can tell, actively seeks out a life that is empty, meaningless, unfulfilling, morally suspect, or cruel. Everyone, I think it safe to say, wants a good life. Yet, if meaning, flourishing, moral rectitude, and kindness are such precious commodities it may be that they sometimes seem so rare. Everyone wants a good life, however we want to characterize it, but it so often appears that very few people successfully accomplish it. This is not simply because reality sometimes seems geared toward thwarting goodness; humans frequently get in their own way in their attempts to achieve the good life. We make poor decisions based on dodgy information, we act in ways contrary to our own best judgments, we violate our principles and moral scruples. In short, we are often our own worst enemies in our attempts to live well.

The philosopher's bet is that developing a coherent view of the universe and our place in it, that is to say, learning how to be philosophical and think philosophically, makes for better prospects for a good life. Recall that we have been defining the philosophical life as *learning how to ask the right questions*—understood from the perspective of *epistemology* as developing beliefs that are true and reasonably justified—*in order to reach a clearer picture of reality*—considered from the perspective of *metaphysics* as the ability to distinguish between reality and appearances—*so as to live in accord with the way things are*—the aim of moral philosophy or *ethics*, the subject of this chapter. Ethics in its broadest conception, then, is the philosophical investigation of the good life, the study of living well and how to do it. It is about discerning the nature of the good life and developing the ability to make judgments about the path to it.

Broadly speaking, there are three types of distinctions we can make concerning the good life: we can distinguish between good and bad persons, right and wrong actions, and moral and immoral motives. When we attend to the difference between *good and bad persons*, the focus is on persons as agents and what makes them morally praiseworthy or condemnable. The key to these types of judgments typically falls on the kinds of character that ought to be cultivated, the personal traits that make a good person good and a bad person bad. When we shift our attention to the difference between *right and wrong actions*, we focus on the nature of actions themselves and what gives some kinds of actions the quality of "fittingness" to a situation and what makes other kinds of actions unfitting. Such judgments frequently, though not always, highlight the consequences of actions, whether those outcomes were positive or negative, and what made them so. Focusing on the distinction between *moral and immoral motives* shifts attention from the actions themselves to the reasons or intentions behind the actions. Among the relevant questions we can ask are whether the motivations behind an action are pure or impure, altruistic or selfish, wholesome or unwholesome. While it is frequently the case that these different types of judgments line up in significant ways—we frequently judge good persons to be those who act rightly from pure motives and bad persons to be those who act wrongly and with immoral motives—the different foci "seat" the relevant ethical considerations in a different place: the character of the person, the nature of the action, or the quality of the motive. A moral philosophy or an ethical theory aims at a coherent and systematic treatment of the good life and how to achieve it, typically by focusing attention on one type of judgment.[1] We do well to take some time to address different kinds of ethical theories.

Perhaps the earliest type of ethical theory to develop in Western philosophy is *virtue ethics*. The preeminent figure in the development of virtue ethics is the Ancient Greek philosopher Aristotle whom we have encountered several times already. Aristotle, recall, argued that all human beings seek happiness and that the happy life is a virtuous life because only virtue is final and self-sufficient. Recall also that he characterized virtue as an activity of the soul. What he meant by this, in essence, is that the virtues are character traits or personal dispositions that must be developed and perfected through habituation to become guides for living. We are not born virtuous creatures, rather *becoming virtuous* is an arduous process of learning the meaning of the virtues and how to apply them, and then developing them as a part of one's nature. The *virtuous person* is one who has incorporated the virtues into her way of living. In this sense, the seat of moral concern is in the character of the individual; the focus of judgment is on good and bad persons. What, then, are the virtues Aristotle thinks central to living well?

He offers an extensive catalogue of virtues divided into two kinds: moral virtues and intellectual virtues. Though Aristotle thought the philosophical life was the best kind of life, and thus no life was truly happy that did not include the *intellectual* virtues—technical knowledge, practical wisdom (ability to discern the means necessary to achieve a good life), scientific knowledge, intuitive reason (knowledge of scientific principles), and philosophical wisdom—virtue ethicists have devoted most attention to his list of the *moral* virtues. They will be the focus of this brief treatment. The moral virtues are:

1. Courage
2. Temperance, or moderation in the enjoyment of physical pleasures
3. Liberality, or willingness to use one's means for the welfare of others

4. Magnificence, or a tasteful extravagance in one's mode of living (provided one has the means to display such extravagance)
5. Pride in the proper degree (that is, neither vainglorious nor unduly humble)
6. Patience, or good temper and slowness to anger
7. Friendliness, or agreeableness in one's intercourse with others
8. Truthfulness or honesty
9. Tactfulness in displaying one's wit
10. Shame, or a fear of dishonor and disgrace
11. Justice

(These virtues deserve more explanation than space allows here; Aristotle's extensive treatment of each of the moral virtues can be found in *Nicomachean Ethics*, books II–IV. We will focus here on the broader outline of the virtuous life.)

The good person, in Aristotle's account, is the one who has come to understand the virtues, how they fit together, and habituated them into her general way of life. This is no easy task since it is not a matter of cultivating several of the virtues; the truly virtuous person must have cultivated *all* the virtues together. Additionally, it is not merely a matter of understanding what the virtues are, but of understanding how they apply to one's individual personality. Aristotle argues that a virtuous disposition lies in a mean, sometimes called the "Golden Mean," between two extremes; at one extreme is a deficiency in the disposition and on the other an excess. For example, the virtue of courage lies in a mean between the deficiency of cowardice and the excess of rashness; the virtue of liberality lies in a mean between stinginess and profligacy. Determining the mean is not merely a mathematical calculation, for where the proper mean falls depends on the individual. In other words, the virtue of courage looks different for a strong individual than it does for a weak one; liberality looks different for one with modest means than for one who is wealthy. And, the virtue of magnificence Aristotle reserves for those with the means to live extravagantly. Aristotle concludes, "Virtue, then, is a state of character concerned with choice, lying in a mean, i.e., a mean relative to us, this being determined by a rational principle, and by that principle by which the man of practical wisdom would determine it."[2] (It seems, therefore, that at least one of the intellectual virtues, practical wisdom, is indispensable to the virtuous life.) In other words, the virtuous person is one who has cultivated all the virtues in the proper way such that they shape her choices and her manner of living.

Some of the Aristotelian virtues may seem a bit strange from our contemporary perspective. While some of the virtues—courage, temperance, patience, and justice (sometimes called the *cardinal* virtues)—clearly seem to fit the bill, others like magnificence, tact, and shame seem odd. Some of this has to do with the way Aristotle conceives of the good life. Aristotle's ethics is a version of *eudaimonistic* ethics. (Most of the ancient and Hellenistic philosophies we have encountered are versions of *eudaimonistic* ethics.) Virtues are the means to a good life, that is, a happy life, *for the individual*. The goal of cultivating the virtues is, for Aristotle, *individual* flourishing. While some of the virtues, justice above all, have a broader aim of securing the good for others, it remains the case that Aristotelian virtue ethics is concerned primarily with the good of the individual virtuous person. The terms "ethics" and "morality" have come to signify a broader arena of concern, one for the general good and not merely the good of the individual. Other types of ethical theory press into this broader arena of concern.

Consequentialist ethical theories shift the focus of attention from the character of the individual and the judgment of what makes a person good or bad to the quality of actions and their consequences. Right actions are those that produce benefits, not just for the individual but for the broader community of individuals; wrong actions are those that have harmful consequences. A strength of these kinds of theories, consequentialists argue, is that they shy away from things that are difficult to observe, like individual character and personal intentions, and focus on effects that are observable and measurable.

One of the most explicitly consequentialist ethical theories is the type of *utilitarian* theory proposed by the British philosopher, Jeremy Bentham (1748–1832). Bentham offered his own kind of *eudaimonistic* ethics, arguing that human beings naturally seek happiness, but, unlike Aristotle, he offered a more Epicurean account of happiness: happiness is pleasure and the absence of pain. Bentham argued that the basic motivational structure of human nature, like all sentient nature, is the pursuit of pleasure and the avoidance of pain; all other higher intentionality arises out of this basic motivational structure. Unlike Epicurus, however, who distinguished between higher, stable types of pleasure—like friendship and contemplation of the universe—and lower, mobile types of pleasure that were fleeting and ultimately unsatisfying, Bentham conceived pleasure as a kind of commodity that could be measured. There is very little difference in the quality of different types of pleasure, he argued, rather we should think of pleasure as a quantity that can be measured according to its intensity and duration, the certainty that an act will produce pleasure as opposed to pain, the temporal immediacy or delay of the pleasure produced, the likelihood that a given pleasure will produce similar pleasures in its wake, and the purity of the pleasure produced. The most important measure of pleasure for the purposes of Bentham's moral philosophy, however, is its *extent*, "that is, the number of persons to whom it *extends*; or (in other words) who are affected by it."[3] On Bentham's account, the right action is the one that produces the greatest happiness, conceived in terms of quantity of pleasure, for the greatest number of individuals. Bentham is quite explicit about this:

> The general tendency of an act is more or less pernicious, according to the sum total of its consequences: that is according to the difference between the sum of such as are good, and the sum of which as are evil. . . . Now among the consequences of an act, be they what they may, such only, by one who views them in the capacity of a legislator, can be said to be material [vis. of importance], as either consist in pain or pleasure, or have an influence in the production of pain or pleasure.[4]

In this way, the *principle of utility* becomes a prospective guide governing action and a retrospective principle of judgment over the rightness and wrongness of actions: right actions are those that produce or are likely to produce happiness, and wrong actions are those that produce or are likely to produce unhappiness—that is, pain—for the individual and the broader community of individuals. The best course of action, and hence the one we *ought* to pursue, is the one that produces the greatest amount of pleasure over pain for the community as a whole.

Few have found Bentham's version of consequentialism genuinely compelling for several reasons. First, the conception of pleasure as a kind of commodity the maximization of which can be calculated seems, at the very least, an over-simplification of a complex phenomenon. Additionally, the principle of utility, as Bentham presents it, could be used to justify acts we might find morally heinous—for instance, the enslavement of a small portion of the population—if they produce the greatest amount of pleasure over pain for the population as a whole. Finally, Bentham's utilitarian principle pays little attention to factors that many think morally relevant, most importantly, the personal intentions of the agent in performing an action; personal intentions have little to do with determining whether an act is right or wrong on Bentham's account. It is conceivable that somebody acting with malicious intent might act in ways that produce a great deal of unintended benefit for the general community; conversely, an act performed with good intention might produce a great deal of unintended harm. Bentham simply thought that too much of the act, its situation, and potential consequence lies outside of the scope of intention; there are too many factors about the situation and consequence that cannot be predicted. The best that intention can do is determine whether somebody should be held responsible or be punished for the negative consequences of his actions. (There are more sophisticated formulations of the principle of utility; the British philosopher, John Stuart Mill (1806–1873) suggested that the principle of utility be adopted as a general rule governing activity as a whole rather that an ad hoc principle applied to discrete actions. Certain courses of action, Mill argued, simply contradict the rule, most importantly undue infringement of personal liberty. Mill also offered a more complex account of pleasure than Bentham's.[5])

Many moral philosophers have found deeper problems with consequentialist theories like utilitarianism, however. The biggest criticism of utilitarianism is its claim that humans are motivated solely by the pursuit of pleasure and avoidance of pain. It seems inconceivable, for instance, that a being so motivated would choose to act in a way that forces him to forgo pleasures, let alone to submit to pain, even if it could be proven that doing so would produce the greatest possible amount of pleasure over pain for everybody else; in this sense, utilitarianism undermines its own claims of legitimacy. These philosophers argue that human beings, capable of higher functions of reason, have the capacity to rise above base concerns over pleasure and pain and adopt higher, more dignified motives for action, ones that allow for genuinely altruistic, other-oriented actions. *Deontological*, or rule-based ethical theories focus on the character of motives; in doing so, they shift attention to the morality or immorality of those motives.

The earliest form of deontological ethical theory is divine-command ethics. These theories, if we can categorize them as *theories*, posit that the rule that ought to motivate our actions is the will of a divine being as that will is presented in particular commandments. A problem with divine-command ethics is that there is general disagreement about what exactly the divine being commands. Specific commandments are usually drawn from some source of revealed material, usually a holy text like the Bible or the Qur'an; a fundamental problem with special revelations, at least from a philosophical perspective, is that they lack independent verification. Special revelations are self-verifying sources of authority that are adopted by and are foundational for particular communities—Jews and Christians in the case of the Bible, Muslims in the case of the Qur'an. Outside of those communities, revealed commands usually have little traction and, without independent verification, lack appeal. Additionally, if it turns out that the divine being does not exist—the existence of God is itself, most philosophers agree, an object of special revelation and not independently verifiable—then the rule disappears with it. For these reasons, many moral philosophers have not found divine-command ethics very compelling. The trick then is to find a firmer philosophical foundation for the rule governing action.

The dominant philosophical account of deontological ethics is the one proposed by Immanuel Kant whom we met in chapter 3. Recall the high regard Kant holds for the human capacity of reason to think itself past its own limits to gain some sense of things as they are in themselves. That capacity to reason is also what Kant grounds morality on. In one of his seminal texts on moral philosophy, he states:

> Inasmuch as reason has been imparted to us as a practical faculty, i.e., as one which is to have influence on the will, its true function must be to produce a will which is not merely good as a means to some further end, but is good in itself. To produce a will good in itself reason was absolutely necessary, inasmuch as nature in distributing her capacities has everywhere gone to work in a purposive manner. While such a will may not indeed be the sole and complete good, it must, nevertheless, be the highest good and the condition of all the rest, even the desire for happiness. . . . Indeed happiness can even be reduced to less than nothing, without nature's failing thereby in her purpose; for reason recognizes as its highest practical function the establishment of a good will, whereby in the attainment of this end reason is the capacity only of its own kind of satisfaction, viz., that of fulfilling a purpose which is in turn determined only by reason, even though such fulfilling were often to interfere with the purposes of inclination.[6]

This lengthy quote, like all of Kant's writings, needs some parsing out. What he means is essentially this: nature has produced in me a capacity for reason that is instrumental in my ability to understand anything about the world; reason also serves a practical function for me, that of shaping my will and my motivations for acting. While I am naturally inclined to seek my own happiness, however happiness is defined, reason gives me the capacity to deny my basic motives and inclinations if moral concerns demand it. Thus, I am not driven along simply by my inclinations—in other words, my will is not determined solely by the pursuit of happiness and avoidance of pain as Bentham would have it—but I can construct for myself moral duties, adopt higher motivations, seek moral goods that are not self-centered. In short, reason is what grounds my dignity as a moral person. In my moral choices, what I aim at ultimately is respect for the dignity of my rational nature.

This recognition of and respect for my own dignity as a rational creature, however, obliges me to the same recognition of, and respect for, the dignity of other beings who have the same rational capacity. Human nature is characterized preeminently as rational nature. Thus, I am obligated to recognize and respect the dignity of other human beings, Kant argues, to the same degree as I recognize and respect it in myself. Such is the ground of Kant's supreme moral rule, the moral motive that ought to guide all my actions, what he calls the *categorical imperative*: "Act in such a way that you treat humanity, whether in your own person or in the person of another, always at the same time as an end and never simply as a means."[7] Concretely, this means that, in my dealings with other human beings, I am obligated to treat them not as objects for use in the accomplishment of my own subjective ends, whatever they may be, but as beings who have their own ends, their own goals and aims in life. The enslavement of another human being, for instance, would be a supreme violation of the moral imperative because it amounts to reducing him to a means for the accomplishment of my goals and aims.

While Kant's moral philosophy has exercised a substantial influence on Western philosophical ethics, there are nonetheless some profound problems with it. The most pressing problem (beyond the complexity of Kant's prose) is that he offers no insight into what obligations I have toward non-rational creatures. My dog, for example, is pretty smart, but he is not rational. (Every time I let him out in the backyard, he hops the fence; this is not rational behavior because it deprives him of my affections—which I *think* is one of the things he wants in life—when I have to go and chase him down. However, he simply cannot resist his basic inclinations to play with his buddies in the adjacent yards or to chase the two wild turkeys that wander my neighborhood.) Yet, I still feel some obligation not to treat him any old way I feel. Obviously, the fact that I "own" him as a pet indicates that I do not feel the same sort of respect for him as I do my stepson, over whom I exert some authority, at least until he is eighteen years old, but whom I do not "own." What, if any, moral obligations do I have toward my dog and other non-rational beings? This is a critical question in an age of mass extinction and ecological crisis. We can expand this problem out further. Kant, for instance, was a notorious racist and thought that most non-European people did not qualify for full human personhood; hence, they were not due recognition or respect, on his account. (Kant's position on the enslavement of people of African descent was pretty ambiguous and not completely in line with his stance on respect for humanity.) Kant's racism and ethnonationalist blindness aside, there remain some fundamental shortcomings with his theories.

The preceding discussion is not meant to be a comprehensive discussion of moral philosophy, or even a complete treatment of the ethical theories of Aristotle, Bentham, and Kant. My aim, rather, is to point to some of the issues involved in the philosophical discernment of what it means to live well. That no one seems to have offered the definitive account should not be taken as reason to despair over the possibility of ever reaching clarity on the good life. Instead, the continuing vigor of the debate over how we ought to live should be a sign of its importance for philosophical thinking.

Neither Plato nor the early Buddhist philosophers, to whom we now turn, offer a comprehensive and systematic ethical theory like the ones we have touched upon thus far. The whole question of how we should live is central to their philosophical concerns, however. Plato's account of the good life is squarely in the territory of virtue ethics, unsurprising given his influence on Aristotle. While moral philosophers interested in Buddhism have found similarities with all three of the ethical theories addressed above, Buddhist ethics seems not to fit neatly in any of the main ethical theories in Western philosophy. Again, this is not terribly surprising given the different cultural context within which Buddhism developed. Whether the ethical visions of either of these positions is compelling is a question we will address at the end.

PLATONISM: THE FORM OF THE GOOD

Plato's ethical writings are part of his broader metaphysical exposition of the theory of Forms. Recall that Forms are the essences that determine what things are: couchy things participate in the Form of Couch, beautiful things in the Form of Beauty. Plato's Forms are usually understood to be transcendent realities that stand apart from the particular things that participate in and derive their existence from them. While the Forms are the basis for reality, they do not all exist on the same level, but are generally understood to be hierarchically arranged in relation to each other; the Form of Couch would exist somewhat lower in the hierarchy of existence than the Form of Beauty. In general, abstract ideas like Beauty, Justice, Virtue, and so forth, stand higher in the hierarchy of reality and apply to things differently than the Forms for physical objects; indeed, to some extent, we could say that the Forms for physical objects participate in, and as such derive their existence in some way from, the more abstract Forms; we can, for instance, talk about beautiful couches (ones quite different than those in my house). Standing at the very top of the hierarchy, grounding the existence of all the other Forms in a way that is not completely clear, stands the Form of the Good.

Plato discusses the Good in multiple places, but in no place are we given anything like a clear presentation of the Form of the Good and its place in the universe. The most complete picture we get is in *Republic* where Socrates speaks allegorically of the sun as the "offspring of the good." In the analogy, Socrates compares the functioning of the Good in the intelligible world to the functioning of the sun in the visible world; just as the sun's power to shed light on visible objects is what gives to the eye its ability to see, so the Good sheds light on intelligible Forms, allowing the mind to know and understand them. Just as light and vision are *not themselves* the sun but are made possible through the power of the sun, so knowledge of the Forms is not the Good, but is made possible through the power of the Good: "This reality, then, that gives their truth to the objects of knowledge and the power of knowing to the knower, you must say is the idea of good, and you must conceive it as being the cause of knowledge and of truth in so far as known."[8] Even more, the Good is responsible for the very existence of the other Forms, much as the sun is responsible for the generation and sustenance of life in the visible realm; thus, Socrates concludes, "In like manner, then, you are to say that the objects of knowledge not only receive from the presence of the good their being known, but their very existence and essence is derived to them from it, though the good itself is not essence but still transcends essence in dignity and surpassing power."[9] The Form of the Good is neither the knowledge of the Forms nor their essence, but it is nonetheless the case that Forms and whatever knowledge we have of them exist because of their participation in the Good.

The Form of the Good, then, serves in Plato's philosophy as both the epistemological "light" that empowers the intellect to know, however hazily, the other Forms *and* as the metaphysical ground for those intelligible Forms themselves (and hence the ground for the visible reflections of those Forms in particular objects in the material realm). To see how this is the case, it is necessary to look at the different ways in which Plato deploys the idea of "goodness." Generally speaking, there are three ways in which he talks about goodness: paradigmatically, functionally, and morally. The *paradigmatic* sense of the idea of goodness concerns the way in which a particular thing more or less faithfully represents a type. To recognize a particular instance of a circle, for instance, requires that I understand the geometrical figure called "circle" the instance represents, and this, in turn, requires that I have some intuition of the Form of Roundness that determines what a circle is. The difference between a good circle and a bad circle depends upon the degree to which the circle participates in the Form of Roundness. While no particular circle will be a completely faithful representation of the Form, circles that are oblong or angular are decidedly bad circles; those that avoid oblongness and angularity are *good* ones.

Plato also treats goodness as a *functional* concept; in other words, we can speak of something as more or less good depending on the degree to which it fulfills its purpose, which again is determined by the Form of the thing itself. The goal of the activity of animal husbandry, for example, is the domestication and care of animals for human use. The *good* husbandman, then, is one who is proficient in the domestication and care of animals, the one whose animals are fit for the various things they are needed for. A good husbandman fulfills the functions assigned to him well.

The *moral* sense of the concept of goodness is the one that most concerns us, because this sense is the one that deals with the comprehensive end of living well. There definitely are dimensions of the paradigmatic and the functional in the moral sense of goodness: the good person is one who represents more or less the paradigm of what a person should be; while we rarely have a complete understanding of that paradigm, it is often pretty easy to tell when someone has faithfully lived into it and when another has missed the mark. Likewise, the good life is what everyone aims at; it is, in some sense, the ultimate purpose of everything we do, thus, the good person is one who succeeds in fulfilling her function as a person. Yet, the moral sense of the Good cannot be reduced to the paradigmatic or functional senses of goodness because it is more comprehensive; living a good life requires more that copying the life of someone who seems paradigmatic of the good life, and it is a good deal more difficult than mastering a set of skills to fulfill a function. Living well is an arduous task of discerning what the Good demands amid the shifting contexts of actual life; it is not a stable paradigm that can be aped or a well-defined checklist of skills to be mastered. To live well requires that we know the Form of the Good, and here is the rub: in this life, we have a shady understanding of the Good at best. Socrates exclaims that the Good is what "every soul pursues and for its sake does all that it does, *with an intuition of its reality,* but yet baffled and unable to apprehend its nature adequately, or to attain any stable belief about it. . . ."[10] Understanding the Good is like looking directly and unaided at the sun: the thing itself is beyond our capacity to fathom and more often discerned by its affects. No wonder so few people seem to get it right.

And yet, as indicated in the quote above, Plato does think that we have some basic intuition of the Good; the problem is that we have somehow forgotten what we already know about it. The philosopher's role is to reawaken us to something that we already know, even if only in partial and hazy ways. To make sense of how this can happen, we need to return to two ideas we addressed earlier: the immortality of the soul and the theory of recollection.

1. *Immortality of the soul:* The human person is not a single thing, according to Plato, but a composite reality. The human being is a *soul* that has become encased in a material body. The soul is eternal and hence immortal; the body is perishable matter that is sloughed off at death. Thus, Plato argued, the body is ancillary to the person, at best a tool that the soul uses to accomplish its purposes in this life. The problem is that the body is an unruly tool; it has its own proclivities and desires that frequently are at cross purposes with the soul. The soul can, therefore, get caught up with the concerns of the body in ways that distract it from what is of greater importance and that hinder the soul in its endeavors to live well.

2. *Theory of recollection:* It is unclear why the soul became embodied, but what is certain for Plato is that, before this happened, the soul lived a disembodied existence in which it experienced the intelligible realm directly. Thus, the soul knew the Forms, including to some extent the Form of the Good; however, this knowledge became fuzzy when the soul entered material existence. In the worst case, this knowledge lies dormant (the condition of most human

beings), in the best case, it remains as a set of shadowy intuitions that we cannot get hold of completely. This is the reason we so often mistake appearances for reality. In those moments of insight into the nature of things we are recalling past understandings we had as a disembodied soul.

These ideas form the basis for Socrates's suggestion in *Meno* that virtue can be learned but cannot be taught: "If the truth about reality is always in our soul, the soul must be immortal, and one must take courage and try to discover—that is, to recollect—what one doesn't happen to know, or, more correctly, remember, at the moment."[11] In a sense, the soul has already learned what virtue is. Socrates role is not that of teacher, but of "midwife"; his aim is not to impart knowledge that his interlocutors do not have, but to birth understanding that is already there in embryonic form. (Or, at the very least, to birth an understanding that his interlocutors do not know what they think they know.)

The virtuous person, therefore, is one who has become adept at discerning what the Good demands in the various situations in which she lives. It is not a matter of adopting a principle or rule to govern actions in all contexts; there is no principle or rule that can apply to all contexts because each situation is unique. Being just, for example, is not a matter of adopting a rule of justice, something like "treat everyone equally" perhaps, because there are situations in which justice demands that we treat people unequally; the strict application of justice sometimes needs to be mitigated by equity or mercy. This is why being virtuous requires not just knowing what the virtues are, but of knowing how to apply them to one's life; and it is not a matter of applying one or a few virtues, because the virtues fit together into a kind of shifting mosaic. What determines the look of the mosaic in any given situation is the work of the Form of the Good. Philosopher Iris Murdoch explains the role of the Good as such: "The scene remains disparate and complex beyond the hopes of any system, yet at the same time the concept Good stretches through the whole of it and gives it the only kind of shadowy unachieved unity which it can possess. The area of morals, and ergo of moral philosophy, can now be seen, not as a hole-and-corner matter of debts and promises, but as covering the whole of our mode of living and the quality of our relations with the world."[12] Living well is a matter of learning, or better, remembering, how to listen to the Good as it speaks to us out of the whole of our lives.

On Plato's understanding of things, then, the principal impediment to living well is *ignorance*, ignorance of the Good and what it requires of us. The path to the good life lies in overcoming, as best we can and surely imperfectly in this life, that ignorance. Philosophy, as it takes form in dialectical engagement, is the process of pealing back the layers of common presuppositions, peering beneath faulty presumptions, and uncovering our blind spots to get closer to the Good.

BUDDHISM: KAMMA, NO-SELF, AND THE NOBLE EIGHTFOLD PATH

Buddhism offers a much different path to the good life. First, as we encountered in chapter 6, the primary impediment to living well is *suffering*, not ignorance. Suffering is the main problem; while ignorance exacerbates and, in important ways, perpetuates suffering, it is suffering that is the issue. Suffering is an ineluctable and unavoidable factor of life, and this fact may make the prospects for living a good life appear bleak. But, Buddhists argue, there are ways to mitigate suffering in this life, *and* there is the possibility for a complete liberation from suffering if one can master the art of living well. Buddhism presents itself as the pathway to that art.

Remember that, for Buddhists, suffering is not simply (or even primarily) physical pain or agony, but rather a general malaise and dissatisfaction with life. The physical side of suffering is a fundamental and unavoidable part of living; we are fragile, impermanent creatures, subject to disease, aging, and death. Try as we might to ignore these facts, they will eventually impose themselves on us, and our attempts to ignore them may make them even worse. Malaise and dissatisfaction, on the other hand, are attitudes we adopt; they arise out of faulty assumptions about, and unrealistic expectations of, life that yield unhelpful and ultimately self-defeating strategies for living. We are our own worst enemies; mental and emotional suffering cause us to engage in unwholesome actions that beget more suffering. The immediate targets of Buddhist practice, then, are malaise and dissatisfaction and their attendant mental and emotional suffering.

A central, ethically relevant teaching of the Buddha is the doctrine of *kamma* or *karma*. It is important to point out that this doctrine has little to do directly with the final alleviation of suffering; *rather, the doctrine of* kamma *explains the ways in which we are active in the perpetuation of our own suffering. Kamma* means action, and the doctrine explains that human actions have a sort of kammic signature that can be read in the consequences of the actions. Philosopher Stephen Laumakis explains: "Human actions produce outcomes or results that are causally determined by the kinds of actions they are. 'Good' actions produce 'good' effects and 'bad' actions produce 'bad' effects. In general, effects follow from their causes in the same way that fruit follows from seeds. In other words . . . the world and events happening around us seem to follow law-like, regular patterns."[13] The seed/fruit metaphor is important and helps to dispel a couple of possible misconceptions that might arise in the attempt to understand the workings of *kamma*. First, *kamma* is not a kind of cosmic justice system, a metaphysical list of merits and demerits, whereby people get what they deserve. *Kamma* is just one aspect of the system of cause and effect that governs everything else in the universe. There is no "getting what one deserves" in any meaningful sense; everything just happens the way it does. Good engenders good and bad engenders bad just as a particular seed produces a corresponding fruit. Second, kammic results correspond to kammic signatures. In other words, actions are not kammically good because their results are positive nor are actions kammically bad because they have negative consequences. Just as the kind of fruit produced does not determine the seed that produced it, the kammic quality of the act is not determined by its results. In other words, the doctrine of *kamma* is not a kind of crude consequential-ism. Something like intention or motivation is at work in the way *kamma* plays out; the motive or intention with which the action is performed bestows the kammic quality on it; the consequence is a necessary effect of the motive or intention.

We need to be clear here that when we talk about the results of the action, we mean the results *for the individual actor*. A teaching attributed to the Buddha states this in direct terms: "Beings are own-ers of their actions, heirs of their actions; they originate from their actions, are bound to their actions, have their actions as their ref-uge. It is action that distinguishes beings as inferior and superior."[14] While an act may have good or bad results for others, these results are not directly relevant from the kammic perspective (though they certainly do have something to do with the kammic seeds of the actions of those other individuals). The doctrine of *kamma* is yoked to another important doctrine of the Buddha, the doctrine of *rebirth*: the kammic effects of action are not limited to one lifetime, rather they follow the individual from one life to another and, importantly, affect the quality of the next life. Bad action may not catch up to the individual in this lifetime, but it will exert its effects in the next. The cosmology that undergirds the Buddhist doctrine of rebirth is one that is composed of multiple realms, the human realm falls roughly in the middle with higher heavenly realms populated by various kinds of divine beings above and lower realms of animal existence and levels of hell populated by ghosts. Depending on one's kammic inheritance, she may be reborn in a higher divine realm or a lower animal form or level of hell. But even if she is reborn in human form the shape her life will take is dependent on the good or bad *kamma* she accrued in the life before.

It is important to reiterate and emphasize that kammic inheritance does not directly affect the ultimate end of the Buddhist philosophical life, that is, the cessation of suffering. While the doctrine of *kamma* is instrumental in explaining how we participate in the cause of suf-fering, how our actions perpetuate suffering, how the character of our motives can increase or decrease the kind and degree of suffering we must endure, it does not explain the nature and source of suffering. To the point, *bad* kamma *is not the source of suffering, and good* kamma *does not bring suffering to an end.* The source of suffering is existence itself, or more properly, our *attachment to existence*; to the extent that the forces of *kamma* remain active in our lives, they bind us to the source of suffering, that is, the *cycle of rebirth* that keeps us attached to existence. While the accrual of good *kamma* can move us toward liberation from suffering, it cannot accomplish liberation. Cessation of suffering requires not just a fundamental restructuring of motivation and action, but *a fundamental restructuring of our understanding of what we are.*

What we *are* is different than first meets the eye. While the human person appears to be a unitary, self-subsisting thing, the Abhidarmikas argue that this appearance is just a *conventional* view. *Ultimately*, the person is neither unitary nor self-subsisting but an aggregation of aggregates; a person is not a thing so much as an interactive process of five elements, the *khandhas* (or, more technically, *upadanakkhandhas* as we will see in a moment). Those five elements are:

1. Material form (*rupa*)
2. Feeling or sensation (*vedana*)
3. Perception or cognition (*sanna*)
4. Volition or will (*sankhara*)
5. Consciousness (*vinnana*)

Thus, the person is not a unity but an aggregation of the *khandhas*. However, the *khandhas* are themselves aggregates; each is not itself a thing, but an instance of conditioned arising of *dhammas* like everything else in existence. The person, therefore, is not self-subsisting, but a sequence of momentary causal assemblages of basic particulars; I am not a self-subsisting, self-determining "I," but sequences of processes of *dhammas* causally aggregating into *khandhas* causally aggregating into this person here now. As Peter Harvey explains, "Each factor is a 'group,' 'aggregate,' or 'bundle' (-(k)khandha) of related states, and each is an object of 'grasping' (*upadana*) so as to be identified as 'me,' 'I,' 'myself.'. . . . The *upadana-kkhandhas*, then, can each be seen as a 'bundle of fuel'. . . which 'burn' with the 'fires' of *dukkha* [vis. suffering] and its causes. They are the sustaining objects of, or fuel *for*, grasping. . . ."[15] The source of suffering is, in the end, my attempt to grasp together these "bundles of burning fuel" into a thing called a self that I can hang onto; the origin of suffering is, *ultimately* speaking, my attachment to and craving for this ethereal thing called "Self."

The notion that craving, grasping, and attachment are the origin of suffering goes back to the initial teaching attributed to the Buddha: the Four Noble Truths. The first Noble Truth concludes, ". . . in brief, the five aggregates subject to clinging are suffering," and the second Noble Truth concludes that the origin of that suffering is "craving for sensual pleasures, craving for existence, craving for extermination [of pain]."[16] That is to say, we want the things that bring us pleasure to continue and the things that cause us displeasure to end; but, above all, we crave the perpetuation of our own existence. Understood correctly, the first and second Noble Truths explain the fundamental cause and origin of suffering not as pain, loss, aging, and death; these are just facts of existence due to the general impermanence of reality as such. The true cause and origin of suffering is our attitudes toward these facts. Harvey explains:

> We like things to be permanent, lasting, reliable, happy, controllable, and belonging to us. Because of such longings, we tend to look on the world as if it were like this, in spite of the fact that we are continually reminded it is not. . . . Such a distorted outlook means that we continue to grasp at things which, by their nature, cannot *actually* satisfy our longings. Thus, we continue to experience frustration.[17]

The cessation of suffering, the subject of the third Noble Truth, rests, therefore, in overcoming our delusions about reality, letting go of our craving for things that cannot satisfy us—including our aversions to things that cause us displeasure, and giving up our attachments to self.

This is a tall order, and, left to our own devices, it is unlikely any-body would be able to attain it. Happily, the Buddha did not end his teachings at three truths, but left behind a fourth Noble Truth, the path to the cessation of suffering, the Noble Eightfold Path. Think of the Noble Eightfold Path as a practical program of discipline for overcoming the craving, grasping, and attachment that cause suf-fering. The elements of the path are as follows:

1. Right view
2. Right intention
3. Right speech
4. Right action
5. Right livelihood
6. Right effort
7. Right mindfulness
8. Right concentration

The path can be broken into three sections, each presenting dis-ciplines that help us overcome impediments to liberation. Right view and right intention aim at the cultivation of wisdom and the overcoming of delusion that keeps us ensnared in the causes of suffering. *Right view* includes understanding of the Four Noble Truths, at least, but also deeper understanding into the nature and impermanence of all things. *Right intention* aims at instilling the fortitude to renounce our attachments, but also to avoid motives of ill will and to not engage in actions that cause harm. The next three elements represent a kind of moral discipline. *Right speech* involves abstinence from malicious talk, falsehood, and idle chitchat; posi-tively, we might characterize it as gently speaking the truth. *Right action* explicitly counsels avoidance of causing physical harm, steal-ing, or engaging in sexual impropriety; also implied, if not always stated explicitly, is avoidance of alcohol and other intoxicants. *Right livelihood* entails, unsurprisingly, earning one's living in ways that do not break the two preceding precepts. The final three elements are what can easily be recognized as mental or spiritual disciplines.

Right effort entails devoting oneself to the avoidance of unwholesome mental states, motives, and actions (that is, those that generate negative kammic energy) and the cultivation of wholesome states, motives, and actions. *Right mindfulness* requires maintaining consciousness of one's physical, mental, and emotional well-being and remaining aware of one's surroundings such that they do not affect that well-being. *Right concentration* concerns the development of meditational abilities that instill calmness of mind and body.[18] Philosopher Christopher Gowans explains that the elements of the Noble Eightfold Path "are clearly intended to be mutually supportive. . . . It appears that the eight steps are to be pursued not in strict sequence, but more or less together, though at any given time some parts may receive more attention than others."[19] On one level, then, the Noble Eightfold Path is a program for better living; but, on another level, it is much more.

The final destination of the path, and the end of the Buddhist philosophical life, is not just learning how to live better, but the complete liberation from suffering through the attainment of full understanding of the universe and one's place in it. Harvey explains,

> Much Buddhist practice is concerned with the purification, development, and harmonious integration of the five 'bundles' that make up a 'person,' through the cultivation of virtue and meditation. In time, however, the fivefold analysis is used to enable a meditator gradually to transcend the naïve perception—with respect to 'himself' or 'another'—of a unitary 'person' or 'self.' In place of this, there is set up the contemplation of a person as a cluster of changing physical and mental processes, or *dhammas* . . . thus undermining grasping and attachment, which are the key causes of suffering.[20]

The person who has reached this stage, the *arahat*, has brought suffering to an end. She has realized the impermanence of all things, given up attachments to things, including and especially to self, and entered into the state of *nibbana* (also known as *nirvana*). *Nibbana* is that state in which one has been liberated from suffering and, most importantly, from the cycle of rebirth that keeps the individual bound to suffering. Harvey describes *arahats* as "those who are fully enlightened, having ended the final fetters of attachment to any heavenly realms or experiences, restlessness, conceit and ignorance. They have experienced *nirvana* in life, brought *dukkha* to an end, and cannot be reborn in any form."[21] The living *arahat* is still subject to the unavoidable suffering associated with disease, aging, and death; technically, full liberation comes only upon exiting the bonds of existence, but she no longer compounds that physical suffering with the mental suffering of desire, aversion, and attachment. She already has one foot in *nibbana*.

In sum, the real impediment to living well is attachment to the concept of Self. I am, in this sense, a burden to myself; my attachment to the idea that I am a self-subsisting, independent entity engenders a deluded view of reality and fuels dysfunctional and self-defeating courses of action that perpetuate, indeed exacerbate, my unhappiness and dissatisfaction. *I* am, ultimately, the cause of *my* own suffering, suffering I can be liberated from only by getting over myself, by realizing that I am really *No-self*. Such is the state of *nibbana*, the liberation from the burden of self.

POSTLUDE: ON SELFLESS PLATONISTS AND ENGAGED BUDDHISTS

For those of you like me, who think that care of self entails a genuine care for others, that a life well lived involves not only securing one's own good but a robust responsibility to create situations where others can secure theirs as well, Platonism and the early Theravadan Buddhist tradition will be unsatisfying. While it is true that the Platonic account of virtue and the Theravadan account of liberation include other-regarding orientations, those orientations are not interwoven deeply into one's own end of living well.

Plato's account of the virtuous life is almost wholly concerned with individual well-being. Philosopher David Hitchcock explains:

> Plato identifies the virtue of a human being with the virtue of his or her soul. . . . Good human beings—that is, human beings who possess virtue—live good lives in the sense of managing their affairs well. . . . To manage one's affairs well has primarily a prudential rather than a moral sense: it consists in doing and acquiring what is good in the sense of being beneficial for oneself. Thus a soul does its work well when it acts so as to benefit itself.[22]

For Plato, the virtuous soul is the well-ordered soul, the soul that lives according to the Good, the ultimate principle of order. Certainly, some virtues have traction beyond an individual life; the virtue of justice for instance, is not only a principle of order in the individual soul, but a principle of order in the broader society. The just soul in important ways mirrors the just social order, and thus the just person is indispensable to the functioning of society. But a just society, in Plato's understanding, is one that manages its affairs well, one that is organized so as to function smoothly. The Platonic account of justice in no way guarantees that individuals are free to seek their own good, nor does it entail that human beings have a right to resources that would allow them to do so. In fact, Plato's understanding of the perfectly just society entails that some people exist in positions of servitude to others, and some members of the society, namely, women and slaves, are left out of the calculation of justice altogether.[23]

The early Theravadan understanding of liberation from suffering is likewise a wholly individual journey. The goal of the *arahat*, the fully enlightened being, is *nibbana*, liberation from the cycle of rebirth, the process that keeps him in wandering and suffering. Somewhat paradoxically, at least on the surface, the achievement of no-self and complete non-attachment awakens in the *arahat* a profound sense of compassion for others who suffer and an attitude of loving kindness that aims to mitigate their suffering. Indeed, the

Buddha suggests that a genuine compassion and care for others can only exist once one has achieved enlightenment; prior to this, my concern for others' happiness is really concern for my own happiness. But the *arahat's* sense of compassion and attitude of loving kindness in no way commits him to work toward the liberation of others. Indeed, to some extent, the early tradition makes individuals responsible for their own suffering through the doctrine of *kamma*. Buddhist scholar Sallie King explains:

> While the Buddha decidedly did *not* teach that everything that happens to a person in his or her life is the karmic outcome of that person's deeds in previous lifetimes, the Buddha *is* recorded as having said that the particular circumstances of one's birth—one's gender, health, wealth, physical looks, etc.— are the karmic consequences of actions in past lives. The view, then, is that one earned the particulars of one's birth. If one is born into an impoverished family or with a disabled body, this is not just bad luck but a caused and appropriate outcome.[24]

In this reading of *kamma*, the enlightened one is rather conveniently relieved of any responsibility for the suffering of others; it is just a part of the cosmic plan.

I suggest that there are two interrelated tendencies that Platonism and early Buddhist thought share that account for the lack of a sense of the mutual implication of care of self and care for others, and thus make them problematic accounts of the good life and how to achieve it. We have touched on both shortcomings briefly elsewhere; now is the time to address them more directly. First, both Plato and the early Buddhist philosophers devalued the physical world in which we live as illusory and distracting. For Plato, the material world is a mere reflection of the true, intelligible realm; to invest it with any importance is to mistake appearance for reality. For the Abhidharmikas, the world of our senses is a collection of mere conventional realities; to truly understand the nature of reality is to recognize the process of conditioned arising and the fundamental impermanence of things.

Given that the material and the conventional is where we encounter other human beings in their suffering and pain, both traditions urge us to turn away from any robust sense of responsibility for them. Second, Plato and the Abhidharmikas conceive the sources of suffering and the impediments to the good life as individual problems. Plato suggests that individual ignorance concerning the Good is the obstacle to living well. The Abhidharmikas associate suffering with individual delusion and bad *kamma*. In short, neither tradition of thought has any deep sense of social-structural issues that put some individuals at a disadvantage relative to others; there is no sense that these social-structural problems need to be remedied.

I do not think we should blame Plato or the Abhidharmikas for lacking an adequate analysis of social-structural problems or concern with the material condition in which people live, nor do I want to suggest that we abandon them as valuable philosophical positions. They are in this respect a product of their times; attention to social-structural inequities is a recent development in philosophy. I do want to assert, however, that any complete and responsible treatment must address both the philosophical strengths and weaknesses of a position, and to offer a revision if necessary. Happily, such critique and revision has been going on in Platonism and Buddhism for some time.

Iris Murdoch argued that Plato's notion of the Good as a transcendent, universal ground of reality can only exercise moral force if conceived as a "concrete universal" that is embodied in individuals who can call us to responsibility and to love. Alluding to Plato's allegory of the cave, Murdoch explains: "Because of his ambiguous attitude to the sensible world . . . and because of his confidence in the revolutionary power of mathematics, Plato sometimes seems to imply that the road towards the Good leads away from the world of particularity and detail. However, he speaks of a descending as well as an ascending dialectic and he speaks of a return to the cave."[25] If Plato does not focus much on this descending dialectic that puts the philosopher back in touch with the concrete good, Murdoch argues that it is nonetheless there to discover. If we so often find it difficult to see the Good manifest in the world, this is not because it is not there, but because our self-centeredness prevents us from seeing it.

> The self, the place where we live, is a place of illusion. Good-
> ness is connected with the attempt to see the unself, to see
> and to respond to the real world in the light of virtuous con-
> sciousness. This is the non-metaphysical meaning of the idea
> of transcendence to which philosophers have so constantly
> resorted in their explanation of goodness. "Good is a tran-
> scendent reality" means that virtue is the attempt to pierce the
> veil of selfish consciousness and join the world as it really is.[26]

To adopt another of Plato's analogies, we tend to miss goodness in the world because we allow ourselves to get in the way such that we can see the world only in our own shadow and not as it is revealed in the light of the Good. In this sense, living a good life requires getting out the way, getting over ourselves, and attending to others and their needs so that we can recognize (perhaps recollect?) our moral obligations.

Similar revision and reform have taken place in Buddhism. Indeed, the second great school in the Buddhist tradition, the Mahayana tradition, emerged out of a criticism of what could be interpreted as a self-centered element of the Theravadan ideal of the *arahat*. Mahayana Buddhism emerged between the first century BCE and the first century CE. The Mahayanists proposed a different vision of the perfectly enlightened being, the *bodhisattva*. Gowans explains, "The Mahayana texts repeatedly proclaim the superiority of their teaching over previous forms of Buddhism. . . . One of the most common motifs in these texts is a contrast between the *arahant*, who is said to be inferior because he sought enlightenment only for himself, and the bodhisattva, who is said to be superior because he sought enlightenment, not just for himself but for the sake of all sentient beings."[27] The bodhisattva, then, is one who attains *nirvana*, but who then remains in the cycle of rebirth in order to work toward the liberation of other sentient beings; her goal is not just her own liberation but that of others as well.

Another movement in Buddhism has emerged more recently called "Socially Engaged Buddhism." It is difficult to know whether this movement represents a new school in Buddhism, or a common set of sensibilities shared by a number of Buddhists from currently existing schools; the latter is the more common interpretation. Engaged Buddhists have reinterpreted central Buddhist teachings like conditioned arising and *kamma* in light of more contemporary social realities. Speaking of conditioned arising (sometimes called "dependent origination") Sallie King explains: "While the usefulness of the teaching of dependent origination has traditionally been applied to personal spiritual transformation, the Engaged Buddhists see no reason not to apply it to societal transformation as well. Thus if there is something from which one wants to free the world (for example, war, poverty, racism) then one should look to the causes and conditions that bring that reality into being and see what action can be brought to bear to eliminate or alter those causes or conditions."[28] In short, the social-structural delusions that lead to unwholesome social conditions can be thought in terms of conditioned arising in the same way that individual delusions can. Likewise, Engaged Buddhists have rethought the way that *kamma* works to empower individuals to engage in actions that lead to social change.

When urging people to take action, Engaged Buddhists focus on the present and future aspects of karma: one is constructing the future with what one is doing now. Clearly this is empowering; it is the very opposite, in fact, of what Engaged Buddhists say have been earlier *mis*interpretations of karma, which have emphasized what one has done in the past. . . . But if one emphasizes the idea that what one does now determines the future—as is also inherent in the idea of karma—then people feel that the future is open and what they do makes a difference. Such an emphasis changes everything as far as engaging one's life is concerned, be it spiritually or socially.[29]

In short, a progressive understanding of the force of *kamma* provides incentive to intervene to lessen social suffering. Transformation of self involves social transformation as well.

This brief exploration of Iris Murdoch's notion of selfless Platonism and Sallie King's analysis of Engaged Buddhism opens avenues for reclaiming these philosophical traditions for proactive, social-structural change as well as for individual personal transformation. These reclamations also bring the two into closer ideological proximity than might initially be expected.

NOTES

1 A short word about the terminology of "morality" and "ethics": Many ethicists wish to make a subtle distinction of meaning between "moral" and "ethical"; typically, ethics and ethical theory are treated as a more abstract kind of philosophizing while morality and moral theory are reserved for more socially embedded treatments of ethical concerns. While this distinction is an important one, it is not critically important for the purposes of my treatment here, and so I will treat "ethics" and "morality" and their attendant terms as synonyms.

2 Aristotle, "Nicomachean Ethics," bk. II, ch. 6, 1107a, in *The Basic Works of Aristotle*, ed. Richard McKeon, trans. W. D. Ross (New York: Random House, 1941), 959.

3 Jeremy Bentham, *An Introduction to the Principles of Morals and Legislation* (Mineola, NY: Dover Publications, 2007), 30.

4 Bentham, *An Introduction to the Principles of Morals and Legislation*, 69.

5 John Stuart Mill, *Utilitarianism* (New York: MacMillan, 1957).

6 Immanuel Kant, *Grounding for the Metaphysics of Morals*, 3rd ed., trans. James W. Ellington (Indianapolis, IN: Hackett Publishing: 1993), 9.

7 Kant, *Grounding for the Metaphysics of Morals*, 36.

8 Plato, "Republic," 508e, in *Plato: Collected Dialogues*, ed. Edith Hamilton and Huntington Cairns, trans. W. D. Ross (Princeton, NJ: Princeton University Press: 1961), 744.

9 Plato, "Republic," 509b.

10 Plato, "Republic," 505e, 741 (*emphasis added*).

11 Plato, "Meno," 86b, in *Plato: Collected Dialogues*, ed. Edith Hamilton and Huntington Cairns, trans. W. K. C. Guthrie (Princeton, NJ: Princeton University Press, 1961), 371.

12 Iris Murdoch, *The Sovereignty of Good* (New York: Schocken Books, 1971), 97.

13 Stephen J. Laumakis, "The Philosophical Context of Gotama's Thought," in *A Companion to Buddhist Philosophy*, ed. Steven M. Emmanuel (Malden, MA: Wiley Blackwell, 2013), 18.

14 "*Culakammavibhanga Sutta*: The Shorter Exposition of Actions," in *The Middle Length Discourses of the Buddha*, ed. and trans. Bhikkhu Bodhi (Boston: Wisdom Publications, 1995) 1053.

15 Peter Harvey, "*Dukkha*, Non-self, and the Four Noble Truths," in *A Companion to Buddhist Philosophy*, ed. Steven M. Emmanuel (Malden, MA: Wiley Blackwell, 2013), 32.

16 "The First Discourse," in *In the Words of the Buddha: An Anthology of Discourse from the Pali Canon*, ed. Bhikkhu Bodhi (Boston: Wisdom Publications, 2005), 76.

17 Harvey, "*Dukkha*, Non-self, and the 'Four Noble Truths," 37–38.

18 For a fuller analysis of the Noble Eightfold Path, see "Analysis of the Eightfold Path," in *In the Words of the Buddha: An Anthology of Discourses from the Pali Canon*, ed. Bhikkhu Bodhi (Boston: Wisdom Publications, 2005), 239–340.

19 Christopher W. Gowans, "Ethical Thought in Indian Buddhism," in *A Companion to Buddhist Philosophy*, ed. Steven M. Emmanuel (Malden, MA: Wiley Blackwell, 2013), 440.

20 Harvey, "*Dukkha*, Non-self, and the 'Four Noble Truths'," 33–34.

21 Harvey, "*Dukkha*, Non-self, and the 'Four Noble Truths'," 28.

22 David Hitchcock, "The Good in Plato's 'Republic'," *Apeiron: A Journal for Ancient Philosophy and Science*, 19, no. 2 (1985): 66.

23 Plato, "Republic," bks. IV–VI.

24 Sallie B. King, *Socially Engaged Buddhism* (Honolulu: University of Hawaii Press, 2009), 159–160.

25 Iris Murdoch, *The Sovereignty of Good*, 95–96.

26 Iris Murdoch, *The Sovereignty of Good*, 93.

27 Gowans, "Ethical Though in Indian Buddhism," 442.

28 King, *Socially Engaged Buddhism*, 14.

29 King, *Socially Engaged Buddhism*, 165.

Conclusion

Thinking Philosophically and Being Philosophical

The human desire to know and the human capacity to question, reason, and conceptualize make philosophy possible. In this examination of how to think philosophically, we have addressed the major divisions of the discipline of philosophy: epistemology, metaphysics, and ethics. Throughout this exploration, I have tried to show that these three divisions function together; they are not three separate endeavors so much as three movements within a single arc that has the end of living well in mind.

Epistemology—the science of knowledge—raises questions about the nature of knowledge, how we get it, and how much we can know. Knowing something involves forming beliefs about it. However, to qualify as knowledge those beliefs need to somehow correspond to the thing, that is to say, they must be true. False or uninformed beliefs are definitely beliefs, but they certainly are not knowledge. Additionally, we ought to have reasons for holding the beliefs we have, reasons that can be articulated and defended if necessary. One cannot know something by accident. In short, knowledge is the process of forming "justified true beliefs," beliefs that conform to reality and for which we have some evidence. Can we ever be completely certain that our beliefs are true ones? There is probably a bit of uncertainty in all beliefs; our knowledge is always a bit fallible, but the more evidence we can dig up to support our beliefs gives us more justification that they are at least approaching the truth.

Philosophical questions about knowledge are important, because what we want to know about, ultimately, is the universe we inhabit, the focus of metaphysics. It is not difficult to find situations in which the way things appear on the surface is not at all what they are really like. Europeans used to think that the Earth was the center of the universe, that the "heavenly bodies" revolved around *us*. It is not illogical to think so; this is the way things appear from our perspective on Earth. However, the more we began to look into things, the more unlikely this perspective seemed. As Nicolas Copernicus (1473–1543) showed us, objects in the night sky do not behave the way they should if we are indeed the center of the universe. He proposed a radically different picture of things, a picture that places the sun at the center of the universe and the Earth as a planet that orbits the sun along with the other planets we know. It turns out, that Copernicus's initially counterintuitive assertions are more correct than the initial evidence of the senses. (Two notes about Copernicus: First, he knew that his findings would cause an uproar and lead authorities to try to suppress the truth—and possibly persecute the truth teller—so he had the good sense not to publish his findings during his own lifetime; this is a lesson Galileo Galilei (1564–1642) learned the hard way. Second, Copernicus still had a lot wrong—for example, the sun is the center of our solar system, but not the center of the universe, which, so far as we can tell, does not have a center, which is weird to say the least—so there was, and is, still a lot left to figure out.) This finding, that we are not at the center of the universe, radically changed our understanding of things. Indeed, metaphysicians and philosophers more generally refer to this shift as the Copernican revolution, and philosophy has been playing catch-up ever since!

The Copernican revolution changed not just our sense of the universe, but more importantly, our understanding of our place in that universe. While such monumental and comprehensive shifts in understanding sometimes make our lives easier, at least as often they complicate things and raise new questions about how we should live.

Thus, ethical concerns move with metaphysical findings; a transformation in our understanding of the world requires, sometimes at least, a transformation in our understanding of ourselves. Thinking philosophically affects our way of *being*.

It is no overstatement to say that we do not always rise to the challenge. Human beings do not usually like change. We get comfortable with the way things are and generally assume that they will always be that way. We function day in and day out on sets of inherited assumptions, and it frequently takes great effort to move us off those assumptions. Sometimes, people just spout whatever opinions come into their mind and hang onto beliefs for which they lack any kind of evidence. I live in a time when elected officials and unsuccessful candidates can deny the legitimacy of an election in face of overwhelming evidence to the contrary. I live in a time when those same officials can, in broad daylight, urge supporters to rise up and violently overturn those elections, then deny they did anything wrong (all the while continuing to deny the legitimacy of the election they urged others to overturn). Worst of all, I live in a time when those same officials continue to garner the support of a third of the general populace. We seem to have lost the concern for correspondence between what we say and what is true; there is a lot of bullshit out there. It's scary. . . .

The human capacity for self-delusion makes philosophy necessary. The ability to deceive ourselves about the nature of things is the dark side of the marvelous, terrible creatures that we are. If philosophers have not been louder about publicly decrying the degree of lunacy we deal with in our time, it may be that they have lost track of what philosophy has always presented itself as, namely a way of life. Thinking philosophically ought to always move us to *be philosophical*: to be skeptical about what we think we know, to be rational in the formation of our beliefs, and to be logical in thinking through problems. My hope is that this little book will survive the times in which it was written, and that future readers will look back in relieved amusement that we have all gotten a little closer to the philosophical ideal of *asking the right questions, figuring out how things really are, and living accordingly.*

Bibliography

Aristotle. "Metaphysics." In *The Basic Works of Aristotle*, edited by Richard McKeon, 681–926. Translated by W. D. Ross. New York: Random House, 1941.

———. "Nicomachian Ethics." In *The Basic Works of Aristotle*, edited by Richard McKeon, 927–1112. Translated by W. D. Ross. New York: Random House, 1941.

———. "Physics." In *The Basic Works of Aristotle*, edited by Richard McKeon, 213–394. Translated by R. P. Hardie and R. K. Gaye. New York: Random House, 1941.

Augustine. *The Library of Christian Classics: Augustine: Earlier Writings*. Edited and translated by John H. S. Burleigh. Philadelphia: Westminster Press, 1953.

Austin, Emily A. *Living for Pleasure: An Epicurean Guide to Life*. New York: Oxford University Press, 2023.

de Beauvoir, Simone. *The Second Sex*. Translated by Constance Borde and Sheila Malovany-Chevallier. New York: Vintage Books, 2011.

Bentham, Jeremy. *An Introduction to the Principles of Morals and Legislation*. Mineola, NY: Dover Publications, 2007.

Berlin, Isaiah. *The Hedgehog and the Fox: An Essay on Tolstoy's View of History*. New York: Simon and Schuster, 1953.

Buddha. "*Alagaddupama Sutta*: The Simile of the Snake." In *Middle Length Discourses of the Buddha*, edited and translated by Bhikkhu Bodhi, 224–236. Boston: Wisdom Publications, 1995.

———. "Analysis of the Eightfold Path." In *In the Words of the Buddha: An Anthology of Discourses from the Pali Canon*, edited by

Bhikkhu Bodhi, 239–240. Translated by Bhikkhu Bodhi and Nayanaponika Thera. Boston: Wisdom Publications, 2005.

———. "*Culakammavibhanga Sutta*: The Shorter Exposition of Actions." In *The Middle Length Discourses of the Buddha*, edited and translated by Bhikkhu Bodhi, 1053–1057. Boston: Wisdom Publications, 1995.

———. "Extract from the *Milindapañha*, 'Milinda's Questions.'" In *Buddhist Philosophy: Essential Readings*, edited by William Edelglass and Jay L. Garfield, 272–274. New York: Oxford University Press, 2009.

———. "*Madhupindika Sutta*: The Honeyball." In *The Middle Length Discourses of the Buddha*, edited and translated by Bhikkhu Bodhi, 201–206. Boston: Wisdom Publications, 1995.

———. "The First Discourse." In *In the Buddha's Words: An Anthology of Discourses from the Pali Canon*, edited by Bhikkhu Bodhi, 74–78. Translated by Bhikkhu Bodhi and Nayanaponika Thera. Boston: Wisdom Publications, 2005.

Burch, Robert. "Charles Sanders Peirce." Last modified February 11, 2021. *Stanford Encyclopedia of Philosophy*. Sanford University. https://plato.stanford.edu/entries/peirce/.

Carpenter, Amber D. *Indian Buddhist Philosophy: Metaphysics as Ethics*. New York: Routledge, 2014.

Descartes, Rene. *Discourse on Method and Meditations on First Philosophy*, 3rd ed. Translated by Donald A. Cress. Indianapolis, IN: Hackett Publishing, 1993.

Epictetus. *Enchiridion*. Translated by George Long. Buffalo, NY: Prometheus Books, 1991.

———. "The Manual of Epictetus." In *The Stoic and Epicurean Philosophers: The Complete Extant Writings of Epicurus, Epictetus, Lucretius, Marcus Aurelius*, edited by Whitney J. Oates, 468–484. Translated by P. E. Matheson. New York: Random House, 1940.

Epicurus, "Letter to Heroditus." In *The Stoic and Epicurean Philosophers: The Complete Extant Writings of Epicurus, Epictetus, Lucretius, Marcus Aurelius*, edited by Whitney J. Oates, 3–15. Translated by E. Bailey. New York: Random House, 1940.

———. "Letter to Menoeceus." In *The Philosophy of Epicurus*, translated by George K. Strodach, 178–195. Evanston, IL: Northwestern University Press, 1963.

———. "Principal Doctines," In *The Stoic and Epicurean Philosophers: The Complete Extant Writings of Epicurus, Epictetus, Lucretius, Marcus Aurelius*, edited by Whitney J. Oates, 35–39. Translated by E. Bailey. New York: Random House, 1940.

Frankfurt, Harry G. *On Bullshit*. Princeton, NJ: Princeton University Press, 2005.

Gowans, Christopher W. "Ethical Thought in Indian Buddhism." In *A Companion to Buddhist Philosophy*, edited by Steven M. Emmanuel, 429–451. Malden, MA: Wiley Blackwell, 2013.

Hadot, Pierre. *Philosophy as a Way of Life*. Edited by Arnold I. Davidson. Translated by Michael Chase. Malden, MA: Blackwell Publishing, 1995.

———. *What is Ancient Philosophy?* Translated by Michael Chase. Cambridge, MA: Harvard University Press, 2002.

Harvey, Peter. "*Dukkha*, Non-self, and the Four Noble Truths." In *A Companion to Buddhist Philosophy*, edited by Steven M. Emmanuel, 26–45. Malden, MA: Wiley Blackwell, 2013.

Heidegger, Martin. *Being and Time*. Translated by John Macquarrie and Edward Robinson. San Francisco: Harper Collins, 1962.

Heim, Maria. "The *Dhammasangani* and *Vibhanga*: The Perfectly Awakened Buddha and the First Abhidhammicas." In *The Routledge Handbook of Indian Buddhist Philosophy*, edited by William Edelglass, et al., 143–159. New York: Routledge, 2023.

Hitchcock, David. "The Good in Plato's 'Republic'." *Apeiron: A Journal for Ancient Philosophy and Science* 19, no. 2 (1985): 65–92.

Holder, John J. "A Survey of Buddhist Epistemology." In *A Companion to Buddhist Philosophy*, edited by Steven M. Emmanuel, 223–240. Malden, MA: Wiley Blackwell, 2013.

Hume, David. "An Enquiry Concerning Human Understanding." In *Enquiries Concerning Human Understanding and Concerning the Principles of Morals*, 3rd Edition. New York: Oxford University Press, 1975.

Irvine, William B. *A Guide to the Good Life: The Ancient Art of Stoic Joy.* New York: Oxford University Press, 2009.

Kant, Immanuel. *Critique of Pure Reason.* Translated and edited by Paul Guyer and Allen W. Wood. Cambridge: Cambridge University Press, 1998.

———. *Grounding for the Metaphysics of Morals,* 3rd ed. Translated by James W. Ellington. Indianapolis, IN: Hackett Publishing: 1993.

Kierkegaard, Søren. *Concluding Unscientific Postscript to Philosophical Fragments,* Volume 1. Edited and translated by Howard V. Hong and Edna H. Hong. Princeton, NJ: Princeton University Press, 1992.

———. *The Point of View on My Work as an Author.* Edited and translated by Howard V. Hong and Edna H. Hong. Princeton, NJ: Princeton University Press, 1998.

King, Sallie B. *Socially Engaged Buddhism.* Honolulu: University of Hawaii Press, 2009.

Laumakis, Stephen J. "The Philosophical Context of Gotama's Thought." In *A Companion to Buddhist Philosophy,* edited by Steven M. Emmanuel, 13–25. Malden, MA: Wiley Blackwell, 2013.

Lucretius. *On the Nature of Things.* Translated by Frank O. Copley. New York: W. W. Norton, 1977.

Marcus Aurelius. "Meditations." In *The Stoic and Epicurean Philosophers: The Complete Extant Writings of Epicurus, Epictetus, Lucretius, Marcus Aurelius,* edited by Whitney J. Oates, 491–585. Translated by G. Long. New York: Random House, 1940.

Mill, John Stuart. *Utilitarianism.* New York: MacMillan, 1957.

Murdoch, Iris. *The Sovereignty of Good.* New York: Schocken Books, 1971.

Pascal, Blaise. *Pensées.* Translated by A.J. Krailsheimer. New York: Penguin Books, 1966.

Perl, Eric. "The Presence of the Paradigm: Immanence and Transcendence in Plato's Theory of Forms," *The Review of Metaphysics* 53, no. 2 (December, 1999): 339–362.

Plato. "Gorgias." In *Plato: Collected Dialogues,* edited by Edith Hamilton and Huntington Cairns, 229–307. Translated by W. D. Woodhead. Princeton, NJ: Princeton University Press, 1961.

―――. "Meno." In *Plato: Collected Dialogues*, edited by Edith Hamilton and Huntington Cairns. Translated by W. K. C. Guthrie. Princeton, NJ: Princeton University Press, 1961.

―――. "Phaedo." In *Plato: Collected Dialogues*, edited by Edith Hamilton and Huntington Cairns, 40–98. Translated by Hugh Tredennick. Princeton, NJ: Princeton University Press: 1961.

―――. "Republic." In *Plato: Collected Dialogues*, edited by Edith Hamilton and Huntington Cairns, 575–844. Translated by Paul Shorey. Princeton, NJ: Princeton University Press, 1961.

―――. "Theatetus." *Plato: Collected Dialogues*, edited by Edith Hamilton and Huntington Cairns, 845–919. Translated by F. M. Cornford. Princeton, NJ: Princeton University Press, 1961.

Ronkin, Noa. "Theravada Metaphysics and Ontology." In *Buddhist Philosophy: Essential Readings*, edited by William Edelglass and Jay L. Garfield, 13–25. New York: Oxford University Press, 2009.

Seneca, "Letter 65." In *The Stoic Philosophy of Seneca: Essays and Letters*. Translated by Moses Hadas. New York: Norton, 1968.

Sextus Empiricus. *Outlines of Pyrrhonism*. Translated by R. G. Bury. Cambridge, MA: Harvard University Press, 1933.

Suk, Ian and Rafael J. Tamargo. "Neoplatonic Imagery by Michelangelo in Sistine Chapel's Separation of Light from Darkness." *The Journal of Biocommunication*, 42, no. 1 (2018). Accessed July 8, 2022, https://journals.uic.edu/ojs/index.php/jbc/article/view/9331/7506.

Vogt, Katja. "Ancient Skepticism." *The Stanford Encyclopedia of Philosophy*. Last modified, July 20, 2018. https://plato.stanford.edu/entries/skepticism-ancient/

Wachowski, Lana and Lilly Wachowski, directors. *The Matrix*. Burbank, CA: Warner Bros., 1999.

Westerhoff, Jan. *The Golden Age of Indian Buddhist Philosophy*. Oxford: Oxford University Press, 2018.

―――. "Metaphysical Issues in Indian Buddhist Thought." In *A Companion to Buddhist Philosophy*, edited by Steven Emmanuel, 129–150. Malden, MA: Wiley Blackwell, 2013.

Index

Aristotle, 16–19, 30, 53–54, 56, 76n2, 139–41
Augustine of Hippo, 43–44

Beauvoir, Simone de, 71
Bentham, Jeremy, 142–43
Berlin, Isaiah, 31–32
Buddha, 82–83, 104
Buddhism, 81–84, 104
    arahat, 159–62
    Abhidhamma, 84–85, 133,
    Abhidarmikas, 125, 131–32,
        162–63
    bodhisattva, 164–65
    buddhavacana, 84–85, 104–107,
        124
    conditioned arising, 110,
        128–31, 156, 162, 165
    dhammas, 125–33, 156, 159
    Noble Eightfold Path, 106,
        130–31, 158–59
    engaged Buddhism, 165–66
    four noble truths, 104–106, 130,
        157
    khandas, 130, 156–57
    Mahayana Buddhism, 84, 164–65
    nibbana, 159–62
    Theravada Buddhism, 85–86,
        104–109, 132–33, 160–64
    Tripitaka, 84–85

ultimate reality vs. conventional
    reality, 8, 124–34, 156–63
bullshit, 110–13

Chrysippus, 58–59
consequentialism, 141–44
Cynicism, 21–22

deontological ethics, 144–47
Descartes, Rene, 39–41

empiricism, 91–93, 106–107
Epictetus, 17–18, 59, 68–69
Epicurus, 18–19
Epicureanism, 57–72
epistemology, 7–8, 79, 89–94
ethics, 7–8, 80, 137–48

fallibilism, 93–94
Frankfurt, Harry, 110–12

Hadot, Pierre, 3, 11, 12, 21, 60, 66,
    112
Heidegger, Martin, 44–45
Hume, David, 27–28, 38–39, 94

Kant, Immanuel, 41–42, 145–47
Kierkegaard, Søren, 45–46, 49n14

Lucretius, 58, 62

Marcus Aurelius, 59, 64, 69–70

metaphysics, 7, 8, 79–80, 115–18, 170

Mill, John Stuart, 143–44

morality, *See ethics*

Murdoch, Iris, 153–53, 163–64

Pascal, Blaise, 15–16

Platonism, 24, 81–82, 162–66
allegory of the cave, 35–37, 132, 163
the divided line, 94–101, 120–21
the Good, 148–53, 160–66
theory of Forms, 102–104, 118–24, 148–49
virtue, 95, 102–103, 152, 161–64

rationalism, 92–93

Seneca, 59, 63

Sextus Empiricus, 25–26

Skepticism, 25–27

Socrates, 2, 13, 18, 23–25, 35, 82–83, 112

Sophists, 112

Stoicism, 7, 17–18, 58–72, 78

utilitarianism, 142–44

virtue, 17–18, 53–54, 95, 102–103, 139–41, 152, 161–64

Zeno, 58–59